BARON JAY Ltd. **PUBLISHERS**
Faraday Road, Prince Rock, Plymouth PL4 0ST

the SHIP that torpedoed herself

Frank Pearce
a Survivor

© Frank Pearce 1975

ISBN 0 904593 02 9

Printed by P.D.S. Printers
Faraday Road, Prince Rock, Plymouth.

This book is set in 11 pt. Press Roman

This book is dedicated
to those who lost their lives
whilst serving on
H.M.S. TRINIDAD.

I wish to record my sincere appreciation and thanks to my son, Derek, without whose assistance in compiling the text and his construction of the diagrams, this book would not have been possible.

A special thank you to my wife Vera; for her great tolerance and understanding during the long months spent in researching and writing the book.

acknowledgements

The Author acknowledges with gratitude the contributions provided by many Trinidad survivors and those closely connected with the events among whom are:-

Captain L. S. Saunders, D.S.O.
Rear Admiral G. H. Collett, C.B., D.S.C.
Captain H. R. Harold, O.B.E.
Commander J. B. Herapath, D.S.C.
Commander P. R. House, O.B.E.
Commander G. Mann
Captain J. W. Daniels, R.M.
Lt. Colonel R. F. V. Griffiths, O.B.E., R.M.
Captain A. D. H. Jay, D.S.O.
Captain G. H. Roberts, C.B.E., R.D.
Commander F. Bradley, D.S.C.
Flight Colonel Ernst August Roth, German Air Force

Thanks are also accorded to –

Admiral Sir Frank Hopkins, K.C.B., D.S.O., D.S.C.
Commander J. E. G. McKee, O.B.E.
Jack Neale (background material)
Doris Thompson (aid in research)
Pat Coleman (illustrations assistance)
Roy James (photography)
Imperial War Museum (photographs)
Public Record Office,

and others, for their support and encouragement, when writing this story.

contents

	Foreword	xv
	Prologue	xvii
1	A "Colony" is Born	1
2	Farewell Plymouth	12
3	P.Q.8 and the Matabele	25
4	The Threat from Trondheim	42
5	P.Q.13 and the Great Gale	55
6	Trinidad Torpedoes Herself	67
7	Trinidad is Saved	90
8	The S.S. Induna and the U-boat	99
9	Murmansk and the Vital Railway	110
10	Running the Gauntlet	133
11	Trinidad Dies	149
12	The Last Moments	165
	Postscript	179
	Glossary	181

list of photographs

The Captain, Captain L.S. Saunders, D.S.O.	13
The Commander	
now Rear-Admiral G.H. Collett, C.B.,D.S.C.	13
The First Lieutenant	
now Commander J.B. Herapath, D.S.C.	13
H.M.S. Trinidad at Scapa Nov. 1941	19
Icy conditions on the Fo'c'sle	27
The Signal bridge	27
A shot of "Trinidad" from the Walrus plane	50
Some of the crew of the Walrus plane	52
The Pilot and Observer,	
Lt. "Jock" Thomson and S/Lt. Paul House	52
The Walrus at Vaenga	52
Ammunition ship exploding	95
Inside the Kola inlet	95
Convoy passing through pack ice	102
Trinidad in dry dock at Rosta	114
The port side torpedo damage	116
Torpedo damage starboard side	116
The last hours. Three Junker 88's coming in to attack	142
"Trinidad" on fire and sinking at 0120 on 15th May 1942	159
Survivors on arrival at Greenock	174
Survivors on arrival at Greenock	175
The Doctor,	
Surgeon Lt. Cdr. G.H.G. Southwell-Sanders	175

list of diagrams

Fig:	1	Trinidad's movements 26th October 1941 to 7th January 1942	17
Fig:	2	Fleet movements 4th – 14th March 1942	48
Fig:	3	Route of convoy P.Q.13 20th – 30th March 1942	62
Fig:	4	Convoy P.Q.13 Battle area	65
Fig:	5	Cruiser and escorts Battle area – a.m. 29th March 1942	73
Fig:	6	Trinidad's first action 8.43 a.m. – 9.03 a.m. 29th March 1942	74
Fig:	7	Trinidad's second action 9.15 a.m. – 9.42 a.m. 29th March 1942	76
Fig:	8	Position of torpedo impact	79
Fig:	9	The sinking of Trinidad 15th May 1942	144
Fig:	10	Where the four bombs exploded	146

foreword

by ADMIRAL SIR FRANK HOPKINS K.C.B., D.S.O., D.S.C.

This is the story of the birth, life and death of H.M.S. TRINIDAD: written by a man who served in her as an ordinary Seaman throughout her life.

It is in fact, far more than an account of the activities of a British Cruiser in the 1939-45 War. It is a vivid description of the actions and reactions of officers and men, living, fighting and dying in the appalling conditions prevalent in Arctic Seas.

Much has been written about the Battle of the Atlantic, but all too little about the convoys from British ports round German held Norway to the North Russian ports. These convoys carried vital war equipment, including Tanks, Guns, Ammunition, Fuel and Food to our Allies — the hard pressed Russians.

The gallantry shown by officers and men of the Royal Navy and of the Merchant Navy, who knew that to be sunk meant certain death in those icy waters, is something we should always remember.

The lack of co-operation, at times amounting to open hostility, shown by the Russians, made life more difficult and unpleasant for our men than it need have been — and may well have been the cause of some unnecessary loss of British lives.

This Russian attitude is hard to understand and for our sailors involved, hard to forgive. Indeed, this first-hand glimpse of Soviet Russia in the raw, came as an unpleasant shock to the few Communist-sympathisers amongst our men.

I would like to thank the Author on reminding us so vividly of those dark and tragic days. Let us hope that should the call come again; a new generation of young men will be prepared to suffer and if necessary die, to preserve this Country and our way of life.

Kingswear

prologue

We know you not who fight in northern lands,
Who call to us for arms to halt these accursed Huns,
And yet we die who know you not,
To bring you planes and tanks and guns.
But when the victory is won and peace the common lot,
Will you remember us who died or will you say
"These we forgot".

Military equipment had to be sent to the Soviet Union in the Second World War to preserve the Eastern front, without which, the Germans would have been able to turn their full might against the West in an attempt to force a victory. So, ships were diverted from Britain and sent in convoys to Murmansk in Northern Russia. The Germans retaliated by building up their naval and air forces in Norway to cut this lifeline, even though this meant reducing their attacks on the Atlantic convoys.

The Russian convoys were identified by the letters P.Q. when outward bound, loaded; and by Q.P. on their return, empty. They went as far North as possible to avoid the German bases. In winter, most of the passage was by night; but in the summer it was daylight all the way. Once found, a convoy was attacked continuously; by bombs and torpedoes from the air, as well as by U-boats and surface vessels. The convoy might be aided by the white mist which forms near the ice barrier in summer. But the escort was as likely to be hindered by the sea temperature variations; forming layers, which their submarine detectors could not penetrate. With this protection available, U-boats could stay surfaced longer than would have been safe in less extreme waters.

The Russians could not accept any reductions in these convoys, nor were they able to give them much naval or air protection. Convoys continued to be sailed right round the year, regardless of the dis-proportionate merchant and naval losses, until a less vulnerable overland route was opened up through Persia and Caucasus.

Each convoy was defended by a close escort of several destroyers, sometimes of First World War origin, with some minesweepers or armed trawlers. Later this was augmented by one or two merchant ships, equipped either with a heavy anti-aircraft armament or a catapult with a Hurricane fighter, which could not be recovered after launching. Accompanying the convoys, but not so close as to attract U-boat attack, was a stand-off force of two to four cruisers. If German battle cruisers were in Norwegian waters, heavy British units gave further cover and this was how the *Scharnhorst* met her end.

Other books have been written about the overall strategy and command of the Russian convoys. This story is about the officers and men of the *Trinidad* when on the hard fought P.Q.8 and P.Q.13 convoys and the fateful final return voyage — as seen through the eyes of a very ordinary seaman; who is proud to be able to say, "I was there".

Those of *Trinidad* who died, did not, as they say, "lay down their lives".. they died fighting; in appalling Arctic conditions. Against an enemy, who in addition to being numerically superior on, above and below the surface, also had the tactical advantage. A great many of the men were "Hostilities Only" ratings; as the wartime volunteers and conscripts were collectively called. They had had just enough training to perform their duties — in aid of an ally, who has shown no recognition or gratitude since. This was at a time, when, though her fortunes were at low ebb, Britain was determined to stop the Nazis at any cost.

the Ship that torpedoed herself

1

A "Colony" is Born

"Will any one who can use a typewriter, please report to the drafting office".

The message came booming out over the loud speakers as I walked through *H.M.S. Drake,* the Royal Naval Barracks at Devonport, on a hot spring afternoon in early April 1941.

My steps slowed as I considered the announcement, what would I be letting myself in for? I recalled my father's advice, when I had joined the Navy at the beginning of the war. "Don't under any circumstance, volunteer for anything". This request however, seemed innocent enough.

Five weeks earlier, I had returned from a twelve thousand mile voyage, covering Florida, Bermuda, the oil fields of Texas and the colder regions of Canada. The outward journey had proved to be a ghastly experience. With an old gunner who had fought in the First World War, I had joined the motor vessel *Chama,* an oil tanker, at Liverpool Docks as a D.E.M.S. gun-layer; the initials standing for Defensively Equipped Merchant Ship.

Some who read this story, will recall the system that was adopted to train men in the early days of the emergency. Civilians from every walk of life were put through a crash course of gunnery at Cardiff and Barry Island. The six weeks training, which in peace time takes something like five years, churned out hundreds of men, who were then drafted in ones and twos to the D.E.M.S.'s.

I shall not forget the pregnant moment, as the two of us mounted the poop deck at the stern of the tanker and looked at the weapon, which we were expected to fire to frighten away enemy submarines. It was an old fashioned four-inch gun with an out-of-date breech loading mechanism and devoid of any anti-flash shield. The brass plate on the barrel confirmed our worst fears – "Japanese 1901".

A week or two later, well out in a quiet part of the Atlantic, we fired that gun as an exercise. It was a far more perilous experience for us, than it could ever be for the enemy. It was more like an eruption than an explosion and an adverse wind carried the searing flame from the mouth of the barrel, right back over the length of the gun. Choking with cordite fumes, hair singed and clothes scorched, we vowed for the safety of the ship and indeed ourselves, that, as the low flash point fumes, which are expelled from a tanker's ventilation system do not take kindly to hot naked flames, we would never again fire the monster, except in the most dire emergency.

Two days after joining, on a Wednesday morning our tanker in company with 31 other merchant vessels sailed from Liverpool to cross the Atlantic. Our escort was all that could be spared, one small destroyer and two armed trawlers. As darkness fell on Thursday night, the convoy steamed directly into a pack of U-boats. Those who have experienced it, will know the tension and fear that grows, as ship after ship becomes a victim of the torpedoes. Great orange flashes lit up the sky as the deadly tin fish found their targets. Somewhere nearby in the sea were men screaming in the dark for help which could not be given, for in convoy no ship stops. Somewhere out there on the edge of the convoy, periscopes were watching us, carefully selecting their next quarry.

During the daylight hours of Friday, the U-boats kept out of sight; but they were back again by dark to repeat the horror of the previous night. The first light of dawn on Saturday morning revealed only three other ships still with us, drawn close together as if for mutual comfort and imagined protection. After the carnage of the previous night, what had remained of the convoy had scattered and we were now quite alone.

By noon, the warming sun and the unusually calm water of the Atlantic had restored our confidence. We were now nearly a thousand miles out: surely no U-boat could or would operate that distance from base.

How wrong we were. Three hours later our premature optimism was shattered, as we saw the ship on our port beam shudder with a violent explosion. Funnel, bridge and centre deck erupted high into the air as a torpedo smashed into her boiler room. Although our ancient cannon was loaded in seconds, we looked in vain for the ripple of a moving periscope. Increasing our speed and zig-zagging desperately we made a hurried exit. Soon the three lifeboats filled with survivors were mere specks on the horizon. These decisions not to stop were heart rending, but to do so would simply have invited another torpedo attack and another ship sinking, with more men left to die.

Two months later, our tanker loaded with oil made her hazardous return journey quite alone across the Atlantic via Greenland. Successfully avoiding the U-boat concentration, she eventually berthed at Avonmouth Docks. The elation brought on by our safe arrival, was however offset by the news that the *Chama's* sister ship, carrying a similar cargo, had been torpedoed in sight of the Irish coast, disappearing in one tremendous flash, killing all hands. The mood of *Chama's* crew at this time was further aggravated when, after the oil had been unloaded, the Avonmouth maintenance staff threatened to strike unless they were paid danger money to even go aboard the empty tanker.

A few weeks later, I found myself back in *Drake* (or "Guz") awaiting the next inevitable draft chit. Many thousands of men who passed through these barracks will no doubt remember the nickname of "Guz". In trying to trace the origin of the word, it appears it could well be a corruption of the word "guzzle", indicative of the west country man's love of guzzling Devonshire cream. Whatever the meaning, "Guz" it always was and I imagine it always will be.

At this time, hundreds of volunteers and conscripts were arriving at the barracks, facing problems of adjusting themselves to the unfamiliar ways of naval life. The very first day I joined early in 1940, a party of twenty of us were being put through the joining routine; Doctor, Dentist, Clothing Store and so on. Staggering under a pile of clothing, boots, shoes, hammocks, blankets and gas masks, we eventually arrived at the last store. Here a raucous Petty Officer beckoned us to gather round, while he held up a loop of string with a small brown disc attached and addressed us as follows:-

"Now then you lot" he barked, "do any of you know what this is?"

Dumbly we shook our heads.

"Well this 'ere, is what they call a hidentity disc. Now do any of you greenhorns know what you got to do with it?"

Not one of us dared suggest.

"Well, I'll tell yah," he bellowed, "This 'ere is to 'ang round yer neck, so that when yer bloody 'ead's shot off, somebody will know where to stick it back on again."

This macabre remark was accompanied by a roar of laughter at his own so-called joke, that died away as he saw the frozen looks on all our faces. We were glad to get out.

The barracks' routine was, however, boring and frustrating. Breakfast at 7.30, parade at 9.00 before dispersal to various duties. I seemed to have a recurring affinity for old guns, for each morning and afternoon, a small party of us, shepherded by an aged petty officer, dutifully gathered around a couple of old brass cannons at the entrance of the drill hall, to clean them over and over again. A soul destroying operation.

It was therefore in this mood, that the message over the loudspeakers found my state of mind. At least I could think it over. An hour later the message was broadcast again; but by this time I had already made up my mind, so I duly presented myself at the drafting office desk. The Chief Petty Officer in charge assumed a most unaccustomed smile and said.

"Son, you've picked yourself a smashing little job as Commander's writer attached to *H.M.S. Trinidad*. She's a brand new ship, just being completed in the dockyard and you'll be working in a small office in the yard until she commissions".

I've often thought about that smile, because what he didn't say was, "and you've volunteered yourself into the worst naval operation of the war – the Russian convoys". Or, what was soon to receive the nickname "Gateway to Hell".

I eventually located the small office, in a sizeable Nissen hut near No. 5 Wharf and later met the man with whom I was to serve for the next 14 months, Commander G. H. Collett, now Admiral Collett, who proved to be an officer of exceptional qualities, distinguished in bearing and above all, a gentleman.

The following day, I walked across to the nearby wharf and took my first look at the ship in which so much was to happen. She looked a most impressive sight as I neared the gangway. My eyes wandered over the modern bridge structure with its array of radar aerials, the four triple gun turrets and the unusual rows of carley floats ranged along the main superstructure. As I considered the proud lines of this new vessel, I found myself reflecting on the train of discouraging events and different tribulations, through which the cruiser had had to pass to reach her present state of readiness.

The Royal Navy at this time found itself in difficulties due to an inadequate and belated programme of new construction, which in turn stemmed from the self imposed limitations of a naval treaty we had honoured before that. After the First World War international attempts had been made to cut down the size of warships and navies in a political climate favourable to economies and disarmament. The leading powers at the London Naval Conference in 1930, drew up a set of conditions which, though favourable to the Americans who dictated them, were conceded by Great Britain to her loss. In particular she came out of the agreement especially weak in cruisers. She was not allowed to build more than 91,000 tons of new cruisers before 1936 and the total number of her cruisers was not to exceed 50, in spite of the strongest Admiralty plea that the minimum should be 70. Had these 20 cruisers been available at the outset of the war, its whole course would have been for the better, with savings in life and expense far in excess of those in peacetime.

As the inevitability of a war with Germany became apparent an emergency shipbuilding programme was started. This included a new class of six-inch gun cruisers with an 8,000 ton displacement, called the Colony class. Generally they were referred to as the "Fijis", after the first of the class which had been completed some months before *Trinidad*, but still well after the war had begun.

Churchill, brought up in the Dreadnought era of capital ships with large calibre armament, put little faith in ships of this size. At one time he referred to them as "the poor little Fijis" and strongly advised the termination of their building programme. He contended that they could not stand up to Hitler's heavy cruisers and pocket battleships.

Though logical on paper, in practice he was proved incorrect on more than one occasion. The most telling engagement being when the eight-inch guns of the *Exeter*, backed up by the six-inch guns of the *Ajax* and *Achilles*, so mauled the German pocket battleship *Graf Spee* off the mouth of the river Plate, that she withdrew and destroyed herself.

13 Colonies were planned although only 11 were completed. The first 8 had four triple turrets. The experiences of this class under aircraft attack resulted in "X" turret being removed

from four of these ships and extra anti-aircraft armament put in their place. The last three colonies were built with only three turrets and an increased displacement of 8,800 tons. Their masts and funnels were completely upright, unlike the traditional raking ones of other British cruisers. Finally their sterns were cropped square, adding to their already boxlike appearance.

As I studied these features, I noted the two huge hangars in which the two Walrus aircraft would be stowed, built into the superstructure and positioned either side of the forward funnel. Immediately aft of the hangars, the launching catapult deck lying athwartships was identified by the incongruous lines of the attendant port and starboard cranes, which would lie fore and aft when not in use. My eyes looking further aft, took in the secondary armament of eight four-inch guns, located in twin turrets abaft the after funnel and above the port and starboard triple 21" torpedo tubes. Here and there, mounted on the forward and after superstructures, numbers of smaller guns added to the powerful defences against air attack.

There had been two British warships named *Trinidad* before this. The first, dating from 1805 was involved in the Napoleonic wars and the second, an Admiralty S Class destroyer of 900 tons, was completed in 1919 but sold in 1932.

Lady Drax, the wife of the Commander-in-Chief at Devonport, Admiral the Hon. Sir Reginald Drax, laid the first keel plate of the third *Trinidad* in March 1938, driving home the first rivet, afterwards declaring the keel plate well and truly laid. Mrs. Snagge, the wife of the Admiral Superintendent of the Dockyard, Vice Admiral A. L. Snagge, drove home the second rivet and friends of other officers took a similar part in the ceremony.

The skeleton of red steel grew slowly into the shape of a ship. Amid the reverberations of a ship yard, the clatter of windy chisels, the blue flashes of welding arcs and the rumble of tower cranes, the structural components became united. A year and a half later, she could be said to be a vessel, outwardly unimpressive but with the hull complete.

Just six weeks after the outbreak of war, the two million pound cruiser was launched on the 14th October 1939, by the Countess Fortescue, a member of an old and respected West country family.

Another two years were to pass before completion. During this fitting out period, one of the dockyard shipwrights fell into the water while working on the ship's side. The rules require anyone who experiences this sort of accident to be taken to the Dockyard Surgery, stripped of all his wet clothes, examined by a doctor, given a stiff brandy and then sent home in an ambulance for the rest of the day. Following this one genuine accident, the number of apprentices who fell into the water from the *Trinidad* over the next few months became ludicrous; so attractive was the brandy and the time off.

To the dockyard workmen she became known as "The Monument", from having become an almost permanent feature of the yard's landscape, in the three years since work had started. Most of the delays in fitting out had been brought about by the need to correct faults that had become apparent in the running of the first two cruisers of the Colony class to be finished.

During this period, the bombing of the City of Plymouth and the adjacent dockyard at Devonport grew in intensity, reaching a peak in the early months of 1941. On the nights of March 20th and 21st, the Luftwaffe concentrated a total of 293 bomber aircraft over the city, and dropped 346 tons of high explosive and 2,000 cannisters of incendiaries. A month later they were back again for three nights in a row, April 21st, 22nd and 23rd. Each night 120 aircraft pounded this naval port and by the morning of the 24th, they had dropped some 400 tons of high explosive and 2,500 cannisters of incendiaries. These were the main blitzes, although almost every night the city was attacked in lesser degrees.

The devastation was widespread, and to an observer the scene resembled an inferno. Fires raged throughout the city, and the dockyard area of Devonport suffered severely. The glow of fires could be seen over 30 miles away. An acrid pall of black smoke, its base being licked by flames and showers of ascending sparks rose over the area.

The deep roar of the fires was punctuated by the sound of exploding bombs and the continuing barrage of anti-aircraft guns. Above this noise, could be heard the now familiar sound, the steady rhythmic engine beat of the enemy bombers, still being sought by the white fingers of the searchlights as they slowly swept the sky. As each dawn lit the eastern horizon, the sound of aircraft faded, the guns grew silent and the drawn out note of the "All Clear" was heard. The daylight revealed a vast new area of smoking ruins. Life carried on, blitz or no blitz. The people of Plymouth, weary but resolute, climbed out of their shelters, to work another day in shop, factory or dockyard.

Before I turned away from my survey of the new ship, I realised that it was almost a miracle she had ever reached this present advanced state, in spite of the damaging restrictions of a grievous treaty and now the efforts of the Luftwaffe to exterminate her or the yard that was building her.

With the work in the ship so disrupted, it was decided that the final fitting out should take place at Rosyth. If care was taken, the engines were far enough advanced to move the ship from Plymouth to Rosyth. With this in view, the ship was to be stored with sufficient gear for the needs of a steaming crew and running a ship on a five day passage. Owing to the punishment from the intensive blitzes, Devonport Dockyard was not able to supply these stores direct; so urgent demands were dispatched to other stores. Very shortly a most hectic situation developed, with lorries arriving by day and by night from all over the country. Spaces had to be found in the half finished ship and after colossal exertions all the stores were eventually safely stowed away.

Within a week of *Trinidad's* planned departure, the German battleship *Bismark* broke out into the Atlantic; and, after sinking the *Hood* and damaging the *Prince of Wales*, was herself sunk. The *Prince of Wales* was ordered to Rosyth to undergo urgent repairs. This dockyard then stated that they now had enough to do without *Trinidad*. By this time, Devonport Dockyard had licked its wounds and was getting back into trim again, so the order went forth that *Trinidad* was to be completed at Devonport after all.

This created a new set of problems. Firstly, the yard wanted all the storerooms emptied and the gear removed from the ship. The application to the yard for a lay-apart store was countered by the reply that no such space existed. After a heated exchange, a storeroom was however found in the South Yard. This building had no windows left, was on the ground floor and a long way from the ship. With no alternative, the ship was destored and all the gear left with only a prayer to stop any light fingered character taking advantage of the situation. In the event, the majority of the stores were untouched, although such favourites as a clock and some blankets did disappear.

In the weeks that followed, all manner of equipment and fittings were hoisted aboard. Workmen swarmed all over the ship, while officers and key ratings were endeavouring to ensure that they were installed for satisfactory operation at sea. An example of the confusion and disorganisation which arose from time to time during the completion period was the number of boxes, all duplications of wireless receivers already fitted, that arrived labelled, "Replacements for Items lost by Enemy Action". These of course, for a ship which had never been to sea. Understandably however, these situations arose from the magnitude and urgency of the war effort.

Eventually, the latest anti-submarine equipment was fitted, together with the most up-to-date outfit of radar units, which drew attention to themselves by the distinctive shapes of their transmitting and receiving aerials on the tops of the masts.

Looking back, one cannot but regret the delays in the completion of the ship, brought about by the bickering and the demarcation arguments of some of the workmen. The wireless telegraphist's compartments were lined with layers of sheet lead, copper and wood, to make them amongst other things reasonably sound proof. The W/T ratings were regularly needing to have holes through the bulkheads of these spaces to bring leads in for wiring up. The joiners declined to drill these holes as it involved cutting metal, while the sheet metal workers would not cut wood. Finally, Chief Petty Officer Telegraphist Tim Dale had a quiet word with one of the yard foremen, with the result that a power drill was left by accident in the W/T office during a dinner hour and all the holes were drilled by the time the men returned to work. Strange to relate no-one seemed to notice anything, the leads were fed through and the boxes wired up without a comment. A job which had been held up for nearly three weeks over a demarcation dispute was this way settled in an hour. This was in war time, when ships were being sunk and many lives lost through lack of warship protection for the convoys.

During the period before commissioning, when only officers and a few key ratings were involved in the preliminary organisation of the ship, there were problems over private living accommodation: especially for personnel and their wives from other parts of the country, who could only find lodgings in areas well outside Plymouth. This in turn raised difficulties in reaching the dockyard.

A harrowing example of this occurred when one of the executive officers who had borrowed a push-bike attempted to minimise the exhausting effort of walking it up the long steep hill from Kingsand on his way to the Cremyll ferry in the early morning. His plan, which was excellent in theory, was that he should be towed to the top before free-wheeling down to the ferry. Next morning therefore, this immaculately uniformed Lieutenant Commander set off, mounted on his bicycle and connected by two fathoms of rope to a motor-bike. Most unfortunately, it had rained the night before and the amount of mud thrown up the motor-bike was beyond belief. By the time they reached the top of the hill, the mud-enveloped apparition which dismounted from the bicycle could only just be recognised as human by the steady stream of thoughtful and carefully selected invectives flowing forth which comprehensively embraced bicycles, wars, weather and cow-traversed roads in particular.

There was another lighter moment, this time in the yard. The hull of the old warship *Centurion* was being converted into a decoy ship at a nearby wharf. The transformation being carried out, with most of the superstructure merely plywood and canvas. Even the armament, which looked real, was phoney. Much amusement was caused one afternoon, when three dockyard workmen were seen walking briskly along the jetty, carrying a fourteen-inch gun and boasting they acquired their strength from beer. From a distance, the plywood replica, once painted battleship grey, could have fooled anyone. Later on the old *Centurion* was used as a target ship. Very heavy armour plating was secured to hull and superstructure, to withstand the battering from heavy shell fire. She was propelled and manipulated by remote control. Eventually she was used in the invasion of Normandy in June 1944 and deliberately sunk to form part of the famous Mulberry Harbour, which was the temporary bridgehead for the invasion forces.

At the time that Plymouth was being subjected to the mid-April air attacks, *Trinidad* was honoured by a secret visit from the Prime Minister, Winston Churchill. However, the night before his arrival to inspect the new cruiser, an enemy plane flew in low over the dockyard and either by skill or by luck, dropped a bomb straight through the quarter deck. No very serious damage was done, although many of the officer's cabins were badly damaged, which put back the completion date considerably. Not a very inspiring beginning for a new ship and inevitably Lord Haw Haw, the infamous German propaganda broadcaster, made much capital out of the incident.

2

Farewell Plymouth

And so they sail away to war,
No Martial notes to lift the heavy heart,
No pomp or circumstance as they depart,
A quiet going.

The ship was finally commissioned on the 3rd October 1941. After a short dedication service, both the white ensign and the commissioning pendant were hoisted. The Countess Fortescue attended this simple ceremony and presented the ship with a silver bugle.

Captain Leslie S. Saunders took command. His Executive Officer was Commander G. H. Collet, his First Lieutenant, Lieutenant Commander J. B. Herepath and his Gunnery Officer, Lieutenant Commander F. W. Larken. The Departmental Officers were; Engineer Commander A. W. Chisholm-Batten, Paymaster Commander H. R. Harold, Captain R. F. Griffiths Royal Marines and Surgeon Lieutenant Commander G. H. Southwell-Sanders.

That afternoon, the ship's company of some 600 men marched through the dockyard and came on board. All hands, officers and men, then mustered on the quarterdeck to hear their Captain speak to them together for the first time. After this traditional address, normal naval routine can be said to have begun for His Majesty's Ship *Trinidad*.

Most of her ratings were from the West Country, and were serving "Hostilities Only" engagements. For some she was their first ship and these looked for guidance from the older hands, who had already seen considerable service at sea, men who had been in action and also who had survived the loss of their ships. One of the great characters from this category was "Nutty" Newton, the Bosun's Yeoman. No matter how bad things were, "Nutty" always had a twinkle in his eye and a big smile on his face. With a lifetime at sea behind him, culminating in the experience of serving in H.M.S.

13

The Captain.
Captain L. S. Saunders
D.S.O.

The Commander
now Rear-Admiral
G.H. Collett. C.B. DSC.

The First Lieutenant
now Commander
J. B. Herapath. DSC.

Top: The Captain, Captain. L. S. Sauders, D.S.O.
Centre: The Commander now Rear-Admiral G. H. Collett, C.B., D.S.C.
Bottom: The First Lieutenant now Commander J. B. Herapath, D.S.C.

Exeter during her action with the German Pocket Battleship *Graf Spee* off the River Plate, he was able to bear the mistakes of the "Civvy Street" sailors with patience and kindliness. Under a rough exterior was a heart of gold.

And so they came on board, making their way below to the mess-decks, to stake their claim for a locker and a pair of hammock hooks. This would be the only territory they would be able to call their own for only heaven knew how long. For the first few days there was a feeling of hopelessness, wandering around looking for the right compartment while learning how this strange ship was worked; and there was the sadness of being parted from those left behind at home. On top of this was the sheer discomfort brought on by the seeming chaos created by the dockyard workmen swarming all over the ship, finishing off all the last jobs in time for sea trials. Everywhere there was wet paint, grease, chain and electrical cables, fouling one's clothes or wrapping themselves round one's legs when one's hands were full. Without warning open ended hoses might spurt water, orders were being shouted, storing winches springing to life and ashore the reverberation of huge lorries would add to the confusion, as they backed up to unload even more equipment to be stored on board.

Slowly, but surely came system and order. Naval organisation and routine prevailed and on the morning of the 25th October, with a pilot on the bridge, *Trinidad* slipped quietly out from No. 5 Wharf. Engine telegraphs rang and white foaming water churned at her stern as she moved sedately out into the Hamoaze. She was an impressive sight in her new coat of paint and her spotless white ensign just lifting in the light wind. She was over 550 feet long with the top of her superstructure towering 40 feet above the water, her formidable main armament looked menacing in the morning light. A powerful vessel and a welcome addition to the depleted state of the Home Fleet at this time. A satisfactory sight also for the dockyard workers who had built her, some of whom stood watching her move out of sight round a bend in the river.

For the first and last time she sailed through the Narrows, with Devil's Point and the grey buildings of the Victualling Yard at Stonehouse on the port side, while to starboard, on the water's edge, lay the hamlet of Cremyll with the wooded slopes of Mount Edgcumbe rising to westward beyond. Ahead stretched the wide expanse of Plymouth Sound; a safe anchorage, thanks to the long breakwater and boom defences protecting it from the weather and the enemy in the English Channel.

Keeping to the deep water channel, she passed north of Drake's Island and swept in a great curve through the centre of the harbour to pass through the gate in the boom defences. She was then degaussed and, once made safe against magnetic mines, returned to the safety of the Sound to swing and adjust her compasses. By early evening she was moored for her last night at Plymouth.

So urgent was the need to sail, many of the smaller jobs could not be completed. There had been so much rush that the yard electricians did not even have time to fasten the cables correctly with brass clips every six inches. Instead, they bundled them together and tied them up into place every four or five feet. Much of this was done on the way down the River Tamar and out into the Sound, while the preliminary trials were going on.

At 8 o'clock the following morning, *Trinidad* slipped her buoy, swung away and moved towards the gate, which was opened ahead of her by the boom defence vessel. On the starboard beam, the little villages of Cawsand and Kingsand nestled together 'tween their beaches under wooded hills already touched by autumn colours. Away to port across the Sound, the great mass of Staddon Heights stood out darkly, the false walls of Palmerston's Fort silhouetted against the brightening eastern sky; relics of another age, when this country had had to prepare herself for a previous invasion.

The line of the breakwater with the swell lifting and sucking at its granite boulders loomed large as the cruiser slipped past its western end. The lighthouse marking this extremity, though darkened for wartime security, stood like a sentinel guarding the passage. As we passed a flock of sea birds rose up, their cries protesting at this grey intruder.

Against the western sky the headland of Penlee presented itself, outlined by small waves breaking white along the stark shoreline. The creamy wake of the four thrusting screws stretched astern in a receding curve towards the familiar sight of Plymouth Hoe. This green sward, topped by Smeaton's Tower and the by now miniature grey buildings beyond, were blurred by a haze thickened by the pall of smoke rising out of the dampened fires from the air raid of the previous night.

As Rame Head appeared, *Trinidad* altered to the southwest. After she had cleared this headland and was making her way out into the Channel, an air raid warning "Red" was received and "Action Stations" was sounded. Though nothing developed from this alarm, a small army of dockyard workmen appeared from below decks with "What the 'ell's going on?" and were told that they were on their way to Scotland. So great was the danger of leakage of sailing date information to the enemy, that these men had not been told we were finally leaving; lost production being preferable to a lost ship.

Clear of the land our new ship felt the strengthening wind and rising waves for the first time and the great bow started to rise and fall with regular monotony. The first spray whisked over the fo'c'sle bringing with it the early sensations of queasiness.

Looking back, the distant view of our home port soon slipped behind Rame Head, which closed like a door on the city and its surroundings in which so many of us had grown up. For even the coastline now was only a continuous line of headlands whose identities were lost in the hazy sunlight.

By the following morning *Trinidad* was in the Irish Sea, which had been whipped into a fury by the increasing wind. Many of the crew were incapacitated with sea-sickness of a severity only a first day at sea can bring. A programme of exercises to try out the six-inch guns revealed that "B" Turret had only four men out of the twenty seven, who were not troubled by this complaint. One man explained in most confidential terms, that he was violently sick every time he heard the anchor chain rattle. So much so in fact that he had his own private bucket in the turret which was his action station. Evidently his disability had not cut any ice in the barracks drafting office.

As we sailed north, we could see on the port side the vague outline of the Irish coast, with the peaks of the Mountains of Mourne disappearing into the rain laden clouds above. Away on the opposite side, the small Polish destroyer *Kujawiak*, pitched and rolled heavily in the beam seas. In addition to this escort, we also had an aeroplane with us for the initial leg of the journey, so that anti-aircraft firings might be exercised. It was not long before *Trinidad* had a signal from the Admiralty,

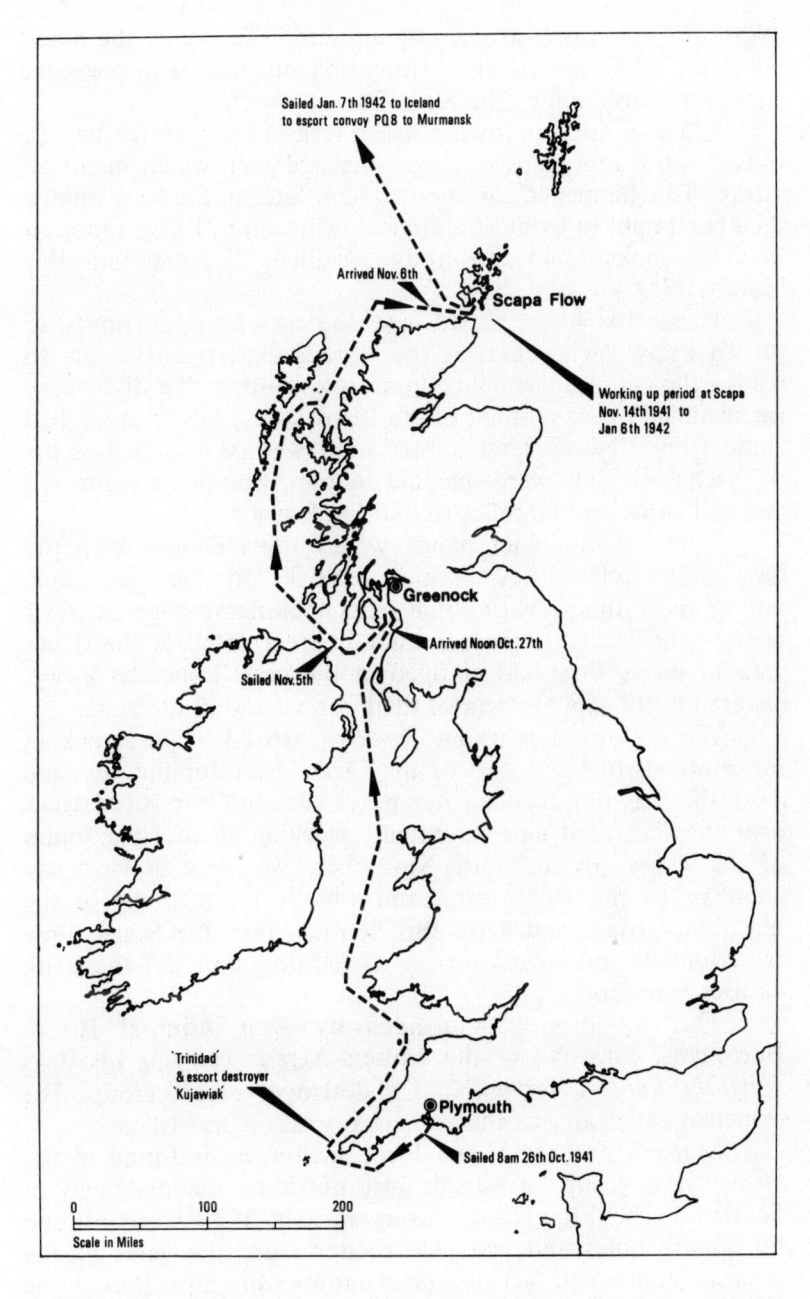

Fig: 1 Trinidad's movements 26th October 1941 to 7th January 1942

"Why are you firing at friendly aircraft?" To which she made the reply, "We are practice firing and our aim is not, repeat not, in the direction of the escort".

Pilots of aircraft towing sleeve targets for practice firings, were always apprehensive about the odd shell which might go astray. This happened on one occasion later in the war, when a shell burst right in front of a target-towing aircraft. It is reported that the shaken pilot promptly signalled, "I am pulling this bloody thing – not pushing it".

These first hours at sea gave the crew an opportunity to get to know each other, as the various departments came to realise their interdependence upon one another. We discovered for instance that a number of our "Hostilities Only" ratings had come from New Zealand, under what was then known as the "Y" scheme. They were splendid fellows, who had volunteered and had come 16,000 miles to join the Royal Navy.

Some of the older hands were quite merciless with the new sailors when they became sea-sick. At the mess table during meal times, with some faces looking very green, they would talk loudly to one another in great detail of the richer greasier meals they had enjoyed in the past. It nearly always resulted in the rapid retreat of the poor nauseated sufferers.

The following morning *Trinidad* arrived at Greenock in the more sheltered waters of the Clyde. Here for the next ten days she was put through her paces carrying out speed trials over the measured mile, eventually working up to a maximum of 32 knots. By the 5th November, we were able to say goodbye to the Dockyard team, who had joined us for the machinery trials, and leave this Scottish port for Scapa Flow to complete our work-up as a fighting unit of the 10th Cruiser Squadron.

This squadron, commanded by Rear Admiral H. M. Burroughs, consisted of the cruisers *Nigeria* carrying his flag, *Norfolk, Kent, Liverpool* and a destroyer escort group. The principal patrol area of this force was west of Bear Island.

Scapa Flow, the Home Fleet anchorage, is found in the Orkneys, a group of islands just north of the mainland of Scotland. The Flow itself covers an area of between 50 and 60 square miles and can give shelter from the gales of the Atlantic and North Sea to a great number of ships. Here in the First World War, the British Grand Fleet waited for the German

H.M.S. Trinidad at Scapa Nov. 1941

High Seas Fleet to come out and fight; and in 1919 after their surrender, the enemy ships came to rest within the Flow and scuttled themselves. The anchorage has three main entrances, situated in the western and southern sides. The more narrow, shallow and tortuous entrances on the eastern side, known as the Holm and Kirk Sounds were thought to be impenetrable. On Friday 13th October 1939, these channels were daringly navigated by Gunther Prien, in the *U.27*, skillfully negotiating the old concrete filled block ships, sunk there in the First World War. The U-boat then torpedoed and sunk the battleship *Royal Oak*, with a loss of 800 men. Immediately following this tragedy, the Prime Minister ordered the eastern entrances to be closed permanently, whatever the cost and effort. The swift tides created immense problems. Vast quantities of concrete blocks were sunk in the waters between the islands making a great highway, stretching from Kirkwall in the north to Burwick in the south and came to be known as the Churchill Barrier.

As we made our way through the Hoxa boom defence into the main anchorage, the scene was hardly encouraging. Barren, low lying and trackless in most parts, the foothills rose gradually onwards to stop abruptly at the high cliffs overlooking the Pentland Firth. This precipitous coastline, in places a 1,000 feet high, is guarded by a pinnacle of rock called the Old Man of Hoy. From the cliff top, a really unique and unforgetably impressive view can be had, if one lies face down and peeps over the edge. From the ship, the only signs of life to be seen on the island of Hoy was a few scattered huts, which, supported by an overworked NAAFI canteen, served as the naval base. Here and there a few cumbersome out-of-place looking oil tanks littered the area.

We passed low lying islands, large and small, brown brackened and desolate, with strange names like Flotta and Fara, Gara and Rysa. To the east, we could make out the Churchill Barrier where it crossed the Holm Sound.

The day after we arrived it was Sunday and gave us our first flutter of excitement. The Chief Petty Officer Telegraphist received a general signal from the Fleet Flagship saying, "Ships are to take individual action to repel aircraft". At this stage, *Trinidad* had not yet received the relevant code book to explain what action the signal required when a ship was at

Scapa. The signal was taken immediately to the Commander, who directed it to be given to the Captain; and he in turn sent for the Gunnery Officer. After a brief conference, they decided it could only mean what it said, namely; enemy aircraft were approaching and ships were to go to Action Stations. The alarm was sounded throughout the ship and a pennant promptly broken indicating that the cruiser was closed up at anti-aircraft defence stations.

Other warships lying in the Flow became very interested indeed and signals were bandied around between battleships, aircraft carriers and cruisers asking what was going on. The Commander-in-Chief at Scapa asked us if we had a radar contact and eventually we had to quote his own signal back to him in explanation of our action. In reply, *Trinidad's* attention was drawn to Home Command War Orders, which we had to admit we did not carry. However the mystery was eventually cleared up when the Fleet Signal Officer came aboard to tell us that we should have been issued with these orders before we left Devonport and the signal was only an amendment to the text. Nevertheless he left with a commendation for the speed and action the new ship had taken. But, as the Chief sadly said afterwards, "I only succeeded in getting all the lads turned out on a lovely quiet Sunday afternoon".

The Flow then became our home for nearly two months, during which time we undertook a concentrated work-up in company with *Renown, Resolution* and *Faulkner*. There were six-inch and four-inch gunnery practices, close range shoots, range and inclination exercises, night encounters, torpedo firings, dummy air attacks and transferring oil to and from a destroyer at sea. All this being an essential part in converting a raw ship's company into an efficient and capable crew in the shortest possible time.

During this work-up period many of the exercises involved shoots at night, so the crew had to master its gunnery quickly. Although the proportion of H.O. ratings was large, they were interspersed with experienced and qualified gunnery rates. Able Seaman Wilbourne was the Trainer in the Director Turret and as such was responsible for the direction in which the whole main armament should be pointing. One night exercise found him vainly peering through the darkness for a towed practice target, when it seemed that everyone else had seen it and were just waiting for Wilbourne to call "Target". As the seconds ticked by so he kept repeating, "Cannot see target" ..... "Cannot see target" ..... At the other end of the intercom, where the Gunnery Officer was waiting, an expectant silence was developing into an explosive atmosphere and the sound of deep breathing was becoming audible. At long last Wilbourne spotted the quarry and shouted "Target". With a blast that threatened to destroy the earphones, another voice roared "And about bloody well time too!"

Though the six-inch shoots directly at targets were a regular feature; throw off shoots at other ships were also exercised to increase efficiency. The projectiles used in this sort of practice were simply steel shells filled with sand, hence were non-explosive. One ship, not *Trinidad*, by accident allowed one of its shells to go badly astray. So far astray in fact, that it hit one of the participating destroyers. A young Lieutenant snatching a late breakfast after night watch, was frozen into immobility with a sausage half way to his mouth, when the stray projectile came crashing through the Wardroom bulkhead and out through the other side.

Life in a triple turret is exacting, often stimulating and sometimes hazardous. In battle, efficiency depends on everyone fulfilling his part in the team. The turret is only part of the whole system, for deep down below are the shell and cordite rooms, with the handling rooms, each with a team of men feeding the hoists which supply the guns.

The following recorded impression of one man who worked below in the magazines, may give some idea of the psychological effect on someone operating in these confined and cell-like spaces.

"When action stations were sounded, I would have to nip smartly down to "A" turret magazine deep in the bowels of the ship, which was just a large iron chamber with a trap door and an iron rung ladder. Timbered shelves and racks from floor to ceiling held aluminium containers filled with cordite and in one section, a fitted flash door enabled one to transfer cordite into the handling department, which in turn served the hoists to feed the guns in the turret. Little could be heard down there, except the varying changes in the engine speeds and the vibrations which occurred in the many changes in direction.

Occasionally, loudspeaker reports were heard giving a commentary of the battle up top, but to the men in these metal dens it was a living nightmare, knowing that if the small hatch cover jammed, one would be trapped. Some of the men suffered from claustrophobia and were fearful and agitated".

"A" and "B" turrets forward of the bridge were manned by experienced seamen gunners and the Royal Marines respectively, whose efficiency in gun drill was a splendid example to the crews of "X" and "Y" turrets aft. These were manned largely by ordinary seaman, conscripted and drawn from all walks of life; plumbers, carpenters, company directors, solicitors, clerks, farmers and many other professions and trades. In the early days of the gunnery work-up, the drill in my own turret "Y", was so poor that I believe the Gunnery Officer nearly had a seizure every time he watched us perform; and one must agree it was pretty bad. A part of the procedure for loading a gun, was that two or three men from the gun's crew should manipulate a long handled mop known as a piasaba. This had to be dipped into a small water tank in the deck of the turret. As each shell was served into the breech, then the duty of these men was to charge forward with the dripping wet piasaba and ram home the shell. A simple enough operation one would have thought, but possibly due to nervousness, because the Gunnery Officer's critical eye was upon them and partly due to the roll of the ship, they invariably managed to get the mop head jammed in the water tank. When they did get it out, they would misjudge the target and slide the thing up the side of the gun. The drill was so bad, that "Y" turret's crew had to have many extra hours of practice to bring them up to standard. At the time, Lieutenant Commander Larken looked on with despair and dreaded the moment that "Y" turret might be called upon to play its part in action.

In those days many of the men, being aware of the insecurity of life amidst the perils of the war at sea, found consolation and spiritual comfort in attending church service, even though it was compulsory.

Altogether the stay at Scapa Flow was not a pleasant one. The weather was atrocious, with heavy gales all the time. It was frequently a case of both anchors down, anchor watch set, steam on main engines, the Officer of the Watch on the bridge and the Captain in his sea cabin close by; when we should have been enjoying some hard won rest in harbour. One particularly bad night, a rather scared looking Officer of the Watch, called the Captain with "Look, Sir, a dreadful thing is happening, the *Edinburgh* is across our bows". And so she was. We cleared the cable party from the Fo'c'sle and immediately went astern, dragging our anchors expecting to part the cables, but they held. With black smoke pouring from both funnels of the great cruiser, *Edinburgh* slowly passed our bow, avoiding a collision by only a few feet. Then, in a flurry of driving snow, threshing from her powerful screws she disappeared from view just ahead. She had dragged while weighing anchor to go on patrol and had given both herself and us a real fright.

This again was an outcome of the pre-war naval conference. In this case the limitation on displacement had brought about a reduction of about a third in the weight of the anchor cable, to keep the ship as big as possible. Without sufficient weight of cable lying along the bottom, the flukes of the anchor would not be enough to keep so large a ship from dragging in a gale. The *Trinidad*, like all her sisters in the Colony Class, was another example of this state of affairs. As one of the first all welded ships, she was so lightly built, that when steaming through heavy seas, one could feel the stern and the bow whipping as the crests of large waves passed under the ship.

The first taste of action stations in earnest occurred when on patrol on one of the few clear days in December. We sighted the masts of a warship on the horizon. Reporting this by wireless telegraphy, which alerted all of the Home Command, we started to chase and rapidly overhaul the strange ship. Action stations were sounded, guns loaded and fingers poised round the triggers. We were about to fire, when the enemy started to flash the recognition signal. She was a thoroughly alarmed United States destroyer on the way to Londonderry from Iceland and nobody knew she was on passage. An anticlimax, but at least it showed that the *Trinidad* was now ready for anything.

3

P.Q.8 and the Matabele

*"And here in frozen Northern seas
Where icebergs lurk midst air so cold
It solidates the breath expelled
And numbs with crude indifference."*

We were now at the end of our working-up period, and by the 7th January 1942, only 8 weeks after leaving Plymouth, *Trinidad* was ordered to take charge of her first convoy to Russia. We left Scapa the same night, setting course for Iceland to pick up convoy P.Q.8.

During the few hours of daylight on the 8th we steered a zig-zag course through a number of floating mines. These had evidently broken away from nearby minefields and marksmen were kept busy trying to explode them with rifle fire. We arrived at Seydisfiord in Iceland on the 9th and immediately oiled in preparation for the voyage.

The following day, we made a slow exit from the fiord accompanied by the large tribal class destroyers; *Somali* (Captain J. W. Eaton) and *Matabele* (Commander A. C. Stanford). A rating from the *Matabele* had been transferred to us just two hours before sailing. Way out to sea we met the little convoy of 8 merchant ships, which had sailed from Hvalfiord two days earlier loaded with guns and tanks for the Russian front. Their escort consisted of the minesweepers *Speedwell* (Lieutenant Commander J. J. Younge) and *Harrier* (Lieutenant Commander E. P. Hinton).

So far the enemy had been slow to react to the introduction of these convoys, which were taking so much needed war material to North Russian ports. Already they had allowed 7 of these convoys to reach their destinations unscathed except for the battering of the weather. This neglect was not likely to last much longer, as already a few surface ships and some dive bombers had been sent to Northern Norway to augment the fearful menace of the U-boats. It was as well that the long hours of darkness and incessant gales moderated the threat of successful enemy action on many days. At this time of year it was 11 o'clock in the morning before a dim grey light came filtering through for two or three hours when it grew dark again for another night.

Slowly the convoy moved along on its journey through the dark Arctic waters, with the escorts moving continuously round the perimeter of the little fleet: each ship fighting its own battle against the everlasting storms, ploughing into the huge seas, climbing up to the foaming crest or dropping into the troughs with $25°$ readings on the roll indicators.

Each night *Trinidad* left the immediate vicinity of the convoy to avoid U-boat attack, exercising night action stations and maintaining as much of a zig-zag course as fuel consumption allowed. The conservation of fuel being just one more factor that Captains needed to worry about on this long passage. Guns and other moving equipment were moved regularly through their full limits to prevent freezing up. On one occasion, the grease solidified in the rotating radar aerial at the masthead, preventing any further scanning operations. Without this vital link in the ship's defence we would get no warning of any attacks developing. In spite of the freezing atmosphere and the incapacitating wind, the Radar Officer climbed the mast and to everyone's relief freed the aerial. How he survived this experience was a miracle.

Below decks men made the most of the time off watch, the younger men usually found some trick to play. One seaman was always smoking a pipe, which only he did not consider repellant. While he was away from his messdeck one morning, these youngsters filled the pipe with match heads and laid a thin layer of tobacco on top of that. When he returned, he lit the pipe and settled down to read a magazine. Suddenly there was a brilliant flash with clouds of smoke enveloping a begrimed and startled face. Apart from scorched eyebrows no harm was done; he was a good sport and within a few minutes was thoroughly enjoying the joke with the rest.

In one of the forward messes the table was embellished during meal-times with primroses, wild violets and a small fern, all growing in a tin. Twice during the voyage the Captain sent someone down to this mess to ask, "May I borrow your garden for my table at dinner tonight?" Able Seaman Jim Harper was the gardener. He had dug them up and brought them

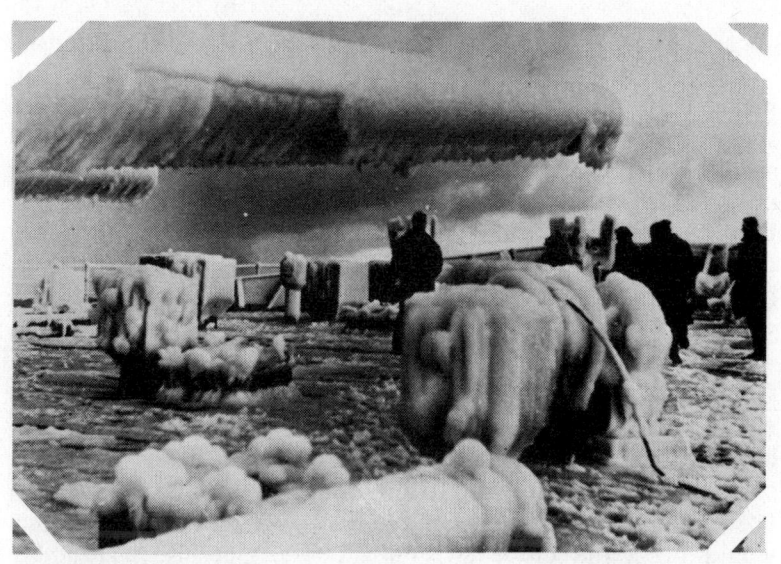

Imperial War Museum *Icy Conditions on the Fo'c'sle.*

Imperial War Museum *The Signal bridge*

Top: Icy Conditions on the Fo'c'sle
Bottom: The Signal bridge

aboard, where they lasted five weeks in spite of the conditions.

Of all times of the year, this was the worst period for man's battle for survival against the vicious seas and freezing spray. In particular this was the most hazardous time for the small armed trawlers, which did such splendid work carrying out rescue operations on stricken ships. Being coal burners they had to carry extra coal in bags on the upper deck to last the journey. This was hazardous early in the voyage, because if ice formed they became top heavy and dangerous in a seaway.

In temperatures which could be as low as 35° below freezing, it would be stupid for a man to place his bare hand on any metal surface. If he did so, he would leave some of his skin behind when he tried to take it away again. It was so cold that eyelashes froze together and the hairs inside ones nostrils froze into little needles; so that a touch on the nose would bring the blood streaming down. One also learned to take shallow breaths, to avoid the pain in the lungs brought about by deeper inhalations.

The ventilation system within the ship was fitted with steam heating, which comfortably increased the temperature. Because of the temperature outside and since the deadlights had to be screwed down over the ports, the condensation in the forward messdecks was excessive. The atmosphere soon became fetid after putting to sea and parts of the inside of the hull grew a thick green mildew. In such conditions with men sleeping in hammocks only 18 inches apart, the slightest infectious ailment could become an epidemic.

I think it would be true to say that the Arctic climate in war time cultivated a background of fear. Fear of what would happen if the ship should be torpedoed and one had to take to the rafts, or worse, how quickly death would come if it meant trying to swim for it. Here in this harsh desolate sea, framed by great ice masses and unpopulated lands, the most buoyant spirit would come to feel isolated from the normal life of the world and become depressed. The pitiless cold, the savagery of the sea, the pervading loneliness and the brutal enemy banded together to undermine the will to endure.

By noon on Sunday the 17th January, with our position $69^o50'$N and $37^o23'$E we were very near the Kola inlet. As the hours passed, approaching the coast, the darkness became more intense. These were the most dangerous waters, where the U-boats gathered in force to intercept the incoming merchant ships. Sure enough at 7.45 that evening, asdic contacts showed submarines to be in close proximity. This however was a job for destroyers, and, having ensured that the convoy was in no danger from enemy surface craft, Captain Saunders swung the *Trinidad* to seaward and clear of the U-boat concentration. These confined waters were no place for a large cruiser to loiter. Hardly had he done so, when, just before 8 o'clock, there was a violent explosion on the port bow. The convoy's leading ship, the Commodore's *Harmatris* had been torpedoed, right on the threshold of Russia, where any other nation might have been expected to have being making some attempt to disperse the submarines that were preying on it's supply lines.

This torpedo had exploded near the bow in No. 1 Hold, where part of the cargo was, of all things, torpedo warheads. Each one of these contained something like 300 lbs. of high explosive. By a miracle all these warheads fell through the bottom of the vessel without being detonated. In the same hold was a large quantity of warm clothes, intended for distribution to Polish internees. These, after being blown upwards through the deck, attached themselves in a most ludicrous fashion to the rigging, just as if the ship was dressed overall with jerseys, pants, scarves and every other conceivable sort of garment, instead of the usual bunting.

It had been an amazing escape for the minesweeper *Harrier*. Seconds earlier her asdic operator had detected something moving towards them very fast, very fast indeed. Instant calculation revealed that this could only be a torpedo coming in on their port beam, far too fast for Lieutenant Commander Hinton to have any chance of taking successful avoiding action. They could only wait, knowing death was very close. But nothing happened; nothing that is until the sound of the torpedo exploding some distance away on the starboard beam. The torpedo had passed directly under *Harrier* drawing 10 feet, just missing the keel and had sped on to blow itself up on the bows of the *Harmatris*, drawing 20 feet of water.

Harrier then went on to escort the convoy into port, while *Matabele* and *Somali* dashed around the group at high speed dropping depth charges. *Speedwell* in the rear hurried to assist the crippled merchant vessel, to find that her crew had abandoned her in two lifeboats. It was clear however that the vessel though down in the bows was not in any immediate danger of sinking; and with care could be saved.

With some apprehension, a number of men volunteered to go back on board and prepare the ship for towing stern first. By 10 p.m. the *Speedwell* with two sweep wires out attempted to tow. After hauling away for some 45 minutes without any progress the starboard tow wire parted, followed by the port one half an hour later. *Speedwell* was back again by 11.30 p.m. ready to make another attempt, only to be told by the party on board the *Harmatris* they had discovered that the explosion in the bow had sent the starboard anchor to the bottom, which accounted for the difficulty in moving her. The situation was further complicated when it was discovered that the steam anchor winches had also been put out of action. The ship was the captive of her own anchor, unable to move or be moved.

Then, while all this was going on, some 4 or 5 miles ahead in the region of the receding convoy, a vast explosion shattered the dark night. An immense sheet of flame, some 700 feet high, shot into the air in an incandescent glare, followed by a mushroom shaped curtain of red hot debris slowly falling back into the sea.

After torpedoing the *Harmatris* the U-boat commander, undeterred by the depth charges, had moved ahead of the convoy, hoping to repeat his earlier success. Some three hours later, nearing the surface in the path of the oncoming convoy, his periscope dimly picked out the hulls of the vessels approaching him and he immediately fired two torpedoes into the middle of them.

It was these that found their target in the *Matabele* and she disintegrated in one enormous flash.

Seconds before, a few miles away, some of the four-inch gun crews in *Trinidad* had seen what appeared to be a searchlight. Perhaps it had been from the *Matabele* or one of the merchant ships and this had shown their position to the waiting U-boat. Clearly however, the torpedoes had found the magazines, for in seconds nothing of the ship remained except for countless floating fragments of furniture and clothing.

Scores of her crew of two hundred had been hurled straight into the sea, but another catastrophe followed. Several of the destroyer's own depth charges, which had already been primed and set to explode at a certain depth, blew up beneath them killing many of those who still happened to be alive. In the confusion that followed, several of the convoy's ships nearby broke W/T silence and interfered with other transmissions. One message, which did come through the jumble of noise to *Trinidad,* were the words ".. Stand by *Matabele* ..."

The *Somali* in the meantime dispatched *Harrier* to pick up survivors. She herself raced round the convoy trying to make asdic contact with the U-boat but without success. *Harrier's* task was both difficult and harrowing. The icy wind, bringing the air temperature down to 28° below freezing, produced an eerie effect with a thin swirling fog, which froze like hoar frost. The decks were a mass of ice and lowering the whaler with the falls frozen solid was a tough and prolonged task.

Eventually the boat was lowered and the men rowed towards the disaster area in intense darkness. As they approached, they found that the sea was covered with a thick layer of oil fuel, which had spilled out from the destroyer's tanks. Steering the boat through the debris, the leading hand was just able to make out numbers of men in their life jackets, floating upright; but a closer look showed them to be quite dead. As the whaler's crew rowed they found the surface littered with men in this gruesome and shocking state, victims of the detonations and the Arctic conditions.

Approaching the centre of the area, the oil became so thick that they could hardly move the boat. The oars were simply dipping into a mass of thick sludge, but getting them nowhere. Not far off they could hear men calling for help from an even thicker layer of this viscous scum; but it was now impossible to go any further and they dare not show any light. Somewhere behind them they heard what sounded like a chorus of faint shouts. With a superlative effort they went astern and within minutes found three men together and still alive. They were enveloped in thick oil and the task of hauling them on board was formidable, for they were all much too weak to help themselves; and in their slippery condition it was difficult to find anything on which to get a handhold. At last it was done and they pulled back to the *Harrier,* much to the relief of the ship's company, because as was said later, "With the ship stopped we were sitting ducks".

Once alongside, there were even greater difficulties in embarking these survivors. This was only accomplished after scrambling nets had been lowered over the ship's side and a Stoker Petty Officer and a Leading Stoker had clambered down and passed heaving lines round the chests of the three men, who by now were almost unconscious. Even then, it was difficult to stop their oil covered bodies from slipping out of the nooses and it took all the strength of these two engine-room ratings to get the inert men up on deck. All three were unconscious by the time they had been carried to the wardroom for medical attention. An hour later one of them was found to be dead. Some hours later after responding to treatment, the other two slowly recovered, only to receive a further shock when in a dazed state they examined their surroundings.

Draped on the wardroom bulkhead was a German ensign. Mistakingly concluding they were prisoners of war in a German ship, they relapsed once more into unconsciousness.

The presence of this enemy flag in a British ship was an outcome of a raid on Spitzbergen in October 1941. Armed landing parties from the *Harrier* and the *Britmark* had gone ashore there to destroy a weather station it was thought the Nazis had established. Search of the buildings showed that the place had only just been evacuated; indeed so hurriedly that packed suitcases and equipment had all been left behind. In the corner of one hut, balanced on a rickety table, an old gramophone still churned out the strains of a German military band, while in another an iron kettle hissed and spluttered boiling water in all directions. Much of the material left behind was collected and brought back to the ships, including the German ensign which had misled the survivors.

By the following morning the two men were recovered sufficiently to discover they were safely aboard a British ship.

Going back in time a bit, *Speedwell's* captain decided that with U-boats around it would be wiser to recover the party from *Harmatris* and carry out an anti-submarine patrol all night, until assistance promised by the Senior British Naval Officer, North Russia, arrived.

At 8 a.m. the next day, the minesweepers *Sharpshooter,* (Lieutenant Commander W. L. O'Mara) and *Hazard* (Lieutenant Commander J. R. Seymour) appeared and took over the anti-submarine screening, while the *Speedwell* transferred the crew of *Harmatris* back on board and prepared to tow. After the anchor cable had been cut to free the vessel, the *Speedwell* towed the *Harmatris* stern first on a course for Tereberski at the slogging speed of three knots.

An hour later a low flying Heinkel III approached from ahead and raked the upper deck with machine gun fire, but without causing any damage or casualties. In the circumstances, Lt. Cdr. Younge sent a signal to S.B.N.O. North Russia for help. He presumed, and rightly so, that further attacks could now be expected and with *Harmatris* in tow he could not take avoiding action. The reply was not encouraging; "Russian aircraft are unable to supply support owing to visibility".

At 2.30 that afternoon another raid developed from another Heinkel, which attacked from astern this time, but by now the *Speedwell's* gunners were ready and waiting. The low level bombing attack was directed at *Harmatris* and as the plane came in for the dropping run, it was met by a concentrated cone of accurate oerlikon and machine gun fire from *Speedwell*, *Sharpshooter* and *Harmatris*. Raked from nose to tail, the aircraft immediately jettisoned its one large and four small bombs astern of the merchant ship. Then after again machine gunning both *Harmatris* and *Speedwell* made a rapid but shaky retreat.

Half an hour later, when only four miles from the Russian coast a small tug arrived and secured alongside *Harmatris* to assist with the tow. Just when it seemed that *Speedwell's* troubles might be over, a mild explosion was felt on her bridge. Then a report came through from the Engine-Room that a tank had burst in No. 1 Boiler Room, injuring three men seriously. The strength of the wind was increasing and ten minutes later both tow wires parted. The tug could however deal with the situation, so *Speedwell* proceeded straight to Polyarny , where the injured men were transferred to hospital.

Trinidad, had entered the estuary at daylight on the 18th, after remaining at sea zig-zagging at high speed, all night. She anchored 6 miles downstream of Murmansk in a place where the curious climatic conditions produced a thick fog, which rose like steam from the river. Once boarded by the Russian pilots, the *Trinidad* was capably and competently conned up river, with only infrequent sightings of posts marking the channel. We never found how this was done, but we soon came to another anchorage off Vaenga, where we oiled from a Russian tanker. Whatever comfort we had taken on the surface from the cover the thick sea fog was apparently giving us was dispelled by the discovery that the tops of our masts were in full view above the top of the fog bank to any enemy reconnaissance aircraft.

In a review of the events of the night before, it was Captain Saunder's opinion that *Trinidad's* sudden alteration of course, just seconds before the *Harmatris* was torpedoed, could well have saved the ship. From the position of the other ships the torpedo could only have missed our bows by a few yards.

A day or two after our arrival in the Kola inlet we took aboard the two survivors from the *Matabele*. They came along to my office to be signed into the ship. They were very young and clearly still suffering from their terrible ordeal. On our return to the British Isles, ten days later, they were transferred to a hospital ship at Scapa Flow, where, we heard, they both died from delayed shock. Only the rating, who had been drafted to us at Seydisfjord at the start of the convoy, survived out of a crew of 200. P.Q.8 had got through, but at what a cost.

During the period of our stay at Vaenga, the rapid falls in temperature astonished us. On the morning of our arrival the air temperature at 4 a.m. was 3° below freezing. At 8 a.m. it was 8° below and by 4 p.m. it was down to 24° below. Midnight showed it at 30° and for most of the following day it had dropped to 35° below. It rarely rose higher than 20° below freezing. Even between decks the inside bulkheads were covered in ice.

Some distance off lay our escorting destroyer *Somali*. Her crew at this time were feeling badly over the loss of all their friends in their sister ship *Matabele*. Captain Saunders instructed the band to embark in the launch and proceed to the *Somali* to cheer up the crew with some light music. The Kola inlet was half frozen inspite of its reputation of being an ice free port. It was very dark and with no lights permitted, everything had to be arranged by hailing between the two ships.

The boatload of about twenty musicians managed to find the *Somali*, where they played dance music for a couple of hours and no doubt achieved their purpose. When it was time to leave, the launch was called and off they went. Half way across they must have encountered a patch of low ice floes, which the boat skidded up until she was high and dry on top of one.

There was cause for alarm in the boat, as she was being carried out of the inlet by a fast moving tide into the sea. The midshipman in charge of the launch eventually hit on the idea of transferring the weight in the boat and shouted, "Everybody come aft and help push off". This they did and inch by inch the boat was edged back into the water. By now however they had lost their bearings and in the snow squalls and darkness could not find their ship. After what must have seemed like hours of calling the correct code word over the loud hailer across the waters, they at long last heard the answering call from *Trinidad* and were soon happily aboard.

As the source of food, equipment and mail, we must have been the most popular ship in the river during our stay. Most of the Royal Navy ships came alongside at one time or other to collect their share of these. *Bramble, Hebe, Hazard, Sharpshooter* and *Harrier* of the little minesweeper fleet took their turn with *Somali* and the submarine *Sturgeon*.

The persistent fog gave us little opportunity to take stock of our surroundings. When it did lift, on one occasion we caught a glimpse of heavily timbered hills, thick with snow, sloping down to the river banks. Here and there were wooden houses almost buried under deep snow drifts.

We were due to sail on the 25th January. On the day before this, in a light snow which was finding its way through the dull grey mist that did duty for light in this part of the world, *Trinidad* was brought alongside a jetty to embark a pitiful company of human wreckage. These were 250 Poles who had spent the previous two years in Russia as prisoners of war after Stalin's invasion of their country at the outset of the war.

As the Officer of the Watch received the Russian guard on the jetty, names were read out and pathetic bundles of grey green topped with long unkempt hair passed slowly up the gangway. Many had tears of joy running down their cheeks by the time they had reached the top and some even fell upon the deck, kissing it again and again. Others just stood still, open eyed and open mouthed, in sheer disbelief that they were free, too overcome to express any sort of emotion.

Once on board they were shepherded into the plane hangar

as this was the biggest available space, and formed into small groups. I spent many hours going from man to man, collecting and confirming the correct spelling of their unusual names. Later, when they were taken below and shared out between the messes, they were made to feel as much at home as the circumstances would permit.

Some were able to tell us that they had been in the salt mines in Siberia and one of the older Poles, who spoke fairly good English, was able to tell us that he had served in the German Navy in the First World War and had fought against us in the Battle of Jutland. His district in Poland was then part of Germany. His ship was sunk in that battle and he had been picked up by one of our destroyers; so he became a prisoner of war in England until the end of that war. Another who was allocated to one of the forward messes showed us his wrists and legs, which were raw through being in chains. For the last six months he had been in solitary confinement, and in darkness except for a little over half an hour every day, when he was allowed a candle. We wondered what his food must have been like.

Four years later, Jim Harper the gardening seaman, was working in Roath Park in Cardiff, when a man passed him, pushing a small child in a push-chair. Several times he strolled by, looking hard before coming over. Standing stiffly to attention, he said, "Excuse me, are you Mr. Jim Harper?" Harper said he was and by then the face seemed vaguely familiar. Suddenly the man gave him an old world bow and went on to announce, "I am Wilhelm Weber of Cracow, I was a Polish prisoner of war aboard your ship *H.M.S. Trinidad*. It is wonderful to meet you again." In the conversation which followed, it appeared that most of the Poles had joined the Polish Air Force and were transferred to their fighter arm at Northholt Aerodrome. Wilhelm Weber rose to a fairly high rank and gained the Polish equivalent of the Victoria Cross.

The following day *Trinidad* steamed out of the inlet escorting the returning convoy Q.P.6, led by the Commodore's ship *Empire Redshank* (Captain Davitt). Apart from a Junkers 88, which sighted us in the brief twilight for a few moments and then lost contact in the darkness, the voyage home was uneventful.

By 30th January we had delivered our convoy into a safe

area and returned to Scapa Flow once more. After oiling we set off for Greenock on the following day, where we disembarked our Polish friends to the accompaniment of much hand shaking and a torrent of unintelligible Polish communications, which were clearly meant to convey their undying gratitude.

Although the need for cruiser support was still paramount, a twenty four hour leave was granted to both port and starboard watches. This provided just enough time for a brief train ride into Glasgow, a meal, a show and a nights lodgings. The following morning we found it had snowed so hard that the trains were at a standstill; so four of us spent our last few shillings on a taxi, which slid most of the way back to Greenock.

A few of the wives and sweethearts of the men came to the jetty to watch the ship sail and wave goodbye. Some hid what they felt, but others gave way to their emotions. All seemed to realise they had their part to play in the struggle to come whatever their premonitions might have been.

At this time some discouraging rumours were filtering through about a breakout of the three German battle cruisers, *Scharnhorst, Gneisnau* and *Prinz Eugen* from the channel port of Brest into the North Sea. If they reached the safety of the Norwegian fiords they would become an additional threat to our Russian convoys.

We spent another week at Scapa Flow before being assigned to Patrol Black. A cold and dispiriting circuit, guarding the area between Iceland and the Faroe Islands. Ploughing through vicious seas, mostly in darkness, every suspicious radar contact instantly activated the clanging alarm bell for action stations. This brought men tumbling out of their hammocks, into which they may have only just fallen, already exhausted by lack of sleep. The constant motion of the ship, as it alternately lifted and fell away from each new wave, did little to accustom us to seasickness or lessen our fatigue. The intensity of these Arctic gales could be alarming, when 60 foot waves came pounding down on the decks of the cruiser. Sometimes the whole fo'c'sle would be submerged until, like a submarine surfacing, the ship would steady herself and emerge with the sea cascading off her, in readiness for the next assault.

Look-outs in their totally or semi-exposed posts had to wear specially heavy and cumbersome protective clothing to face up to the Arctic watches. Once hooded, muffled, gloved, sea-booted and wrapped in numerous layers of thick woollen clothing, their movements could only be laboured and slow. Just to climb companion ways and ladders to reach their duty stations was a most exhausting exercise. It was inevitable, instead of using the longer seaman's route to the bridge positions, especially if he was running late and could do so unobserved, for a man to take the more direct "Officers Only" ladders and passages. On such an occasion, Able Seaman George Morris took a chance. His already laborious and hampered climbing was further delayed by the even slower progress of a similarly over-clothed and hooded figure also making his way in the direction of the bridge. Thinking that this was one of his messmates, he swung his arm to deliver a good sharp blow on the bottom, at the same time calling out, "Chop, Chop, townie, I'm bloody well late already". The figure above slowly turned and looked down — It was Captain Saunders. The utter dismay and astonishment showing in Morris's eyes, must have gone a long way to reveal that the mistake was genuine. Apart from a "Very sorry, Sir", not another word was spoken — the two figures continued their climb. To the credit of the Captain and the relief of Morris, the incident was never mentioned.

To many, the sights and sounds of the life at sea were still unfamiliar. One young seaman on look-out duty, spotting what he took to be an aircraft away out on the horizon, reported to the bridge with some excitement in his voice, "Enemy plane, bearing Green 090". After a moment, a tired but tolerant voice replied, "Observation checked, but aeroplanes do not flap their wings".

A Communications Chief Petty Officer had managed before leaving Devonport, to obtain a hot plate and have it fitted in his office. When on patrol there was always coffee or cocoa on the hob day or night. All this was greatly appreciated by the staff under him and also by those in the office next door, which could be reached by an inter-connecting window. Nor were look-outs forgotten: by some means or other hot drinks found their way to their grateful lips as well.

There were always a few sailors with a special weakness for the extra tot of rum. So, by way of barter, a fair supply of coffee, cocoa and sugar could usually be obtained, however illegal the transaction might be. Many of the officers coming off watch in these icy conditions appreciated the hot drink and were careful not to ask any questions. One officer who did not partake, inquired how coffee and cocoa could always be on call in this way and was frankly told by the Chief, that if anyone started asking awkward questions the supply line would dry up at once. That was the last that was heard of that.

At this time one of our sister ships on the covering force patrolling Iceland had a rather crusty Captain. His son was a midshipman in the same vessel. While on duty as look-out in the crow's nest he accidently dropped his binoculars on to the bridge, just missing his father. The Captain looked up and seeing a midshipman roared, "What on earth are you up to you little bastard?" Then seeing it was his own son's face peering down, quickly added "However, that is no reflection on your dear mother".

The *Kenya* relieved us and we thankfully returned to Hvalfiord in Iceland on the 16th February, to find that the weight of the huge seas had forced "A" turret — weighing hundreds of tons — down into the deck, bending the powerful stanchions placed below to support it. Lifeboats and carley floats also had either been swept away or smashed to fragments in the course of the patrol.

Light relief from this sort of life was provided on one or two occasions for a few members of the crew to go ashore in Iceland, where American forces were based. Fraternisation of the Yanks and the Limies was assisted and stimulated by the swilling down of vast quantities of whisky. These excursions usually ended in some of the crew being first carried to the jetty in an extremely well oiled condition, then laid in the bottom of a boat in a blissful stupor. On arrival at the ship, the bodies were embarked by hoisting them in a cargo net and depositing them gently on deck.

After some months of the privations of Murmansk and escorting convoys there and back, the crew of the trawler *Blackfly* arrived at Seydisfiord for a few hours ashore. A great treat for men who had been on short rations and devoid of outside company for so long. They had not been told that their night ashore coincided with a local religious festival, where it was the custom late on this night to put, on each doorstep, a few fish as a gift offering for the Lord, should he pass by.

That night the *Blackfly* had the best fish and chip supper they had had for months. The following morning the Icelanders meditated on the riddle of the missing fish. It was first treated with awe and mystery, but later with unconcealed rage, when it became clear it was not the Lord, but the lads of the *Blackfly* who had passed by.

The rum issue has a magical attraction for many of the old hands, in barracks as well as on board. Stand in for duty watches and other supplementary benefits could often be arranged for the extra tot. Indeed there was no end to the devices which were tried in order to gain additional grog.

In one shore establishment a very experienced A.B. was placed in charge of the distribution of rum during the frequent absences of the Master-at-Arms. As each man arrived at the table to get and drink his tot, this A.B. would dip the regulation measure into the keg and according to the rules, ostensibly check that the rum was level with the rim, then pour it into the drinking tumbler. What no one seemed to notice was the top joint of his thumb was well and truly immersed within the measure on each occasion. This fiddle repeated many times under the very eyes of his messmates, produced a mysterious but liberal surplus every time, which was promptly disposed of by the old hand and his cronies.

Another irregularity took place at the small Naval base adjacent to the Royal Naval College at Dartmouth. Outside working parties would return at the end of the day, and those entitled would call at the Master-at-Arm's office to collect and drink their tot. On occasions some of the tots were left unclaimed by the deadline of 9 o'clock. Joe Simon, an elderly and well loved Master-at-Arms, would then instruct Able Seaman George Foulkes to take the rum, pour it down the toilet which was immediately outside and flush it away. George, not one to miss an opportunity would comply smartly; but would gulp down the rum then stand to attention while saying, "The King – God Bless Him" and pull the chain. On his return, the conversation would follow the same lines.

"Foulkes, did you get rid of those tots?"
"Yes Master-at-Arms".
"Down the toilet?"
"Yes Master-at-Arms".

"You awful bloody liar Foulkes".

Later on one of the capital ships called in at Iceland to give leave. One of her ratings arrived back on board worse for drink and unsteady. Brought to the quarterdeck he was told by the Officer of the Watch that he was drunk and would have to be charged. Listing slightly the rating replied, "But sir, I've never been more sober in my life". To this the officer said, "Alright Wilson, I'll give you a chance to prove it. I want you to say after me, I can put a hippopotamus in a perambulator". With a slightly puzzled frown, Wilson drew himself up a notch or two and began, "I can put a hipplepopple...pople...pople I can put a hopplepipple...pippa". He stopped, a grin spreading all over his red face and wagging his finger said, "You can't catch me that way sir, 'cos nobody could get a hippo into a bloody pram".

4

The Threat from Trondheim

In the early days of 1942 it had become apparent that many units of the German fleet were ready for sea and able to attack convoys, the main threats coming from the Baltic and from Brest. R.A.F. reconnaissance and intelligence were both agreed that sailings were imminent.

The Baltic was thought to hold some twenty ships, mostly destroyers with large calibre guns that could not be treated lightly. The heavy units in this area were: the pocket battleship *Admiral Scheer*, the heavy cruiser *Admiral Hipper*, four light cruisers, and the new battleship *Tirpitz*, which was to be the first concern of Admiral Sir John Tovey, Commander in Chief, Home Fleet.

The Brest squadron, made up of the battle cruisers *Scharnhorst* and *Gneisnau*, with the heavy cruiser *Prinz Eugen*, had repaired the damage suffered in 1941. In spite of repeated bombing by the R.A.F. in January, the German ships were practically unscathed and were a perpetual threat to the South-West approaches.

With the breakout of the *Bismark* so fresh in his memory, Admiral Tovey was well aware of the consequences of the combination of these two forces. He had to cover all possible outlets in the north and the south-west with only limited forces at his disposal.

In December 1941 a series of British commando raids along the Norwegian coast, while having the desired effect of tying up more German land and air forces in Norway, also convinced Hitler that an invasion was imminent here. Despite the arguments of his naval staff the Führer ordered the *Tirpitz* into Arctic waters and the Brest Squadron to come north.

Instead of the *Tirpitz* sailing through the Skaggerak and the Kattegat, she left by the Kiel canal, arriving in Norway on the 16th January, apparently undetected. Here she released her escort of 4 destroyers to support the Brest Squadron. Not knowing where the German battleship was, Admiral Tovey moved his major units to Iceland to block any thrust out into the Atlantic, and delayed the P.Q.9 convoy long enough to sail with P.Q.10 from Hvalfiord on the 1st February. After 6 days of searching the Norwegian coast the R.A.F. found the *Tirpitz,* heavily camouflaged at anchor in Trondheim. From then on convoys to and from Russia could not be allowed to converge on the danger area between Jan Mayen and Bear Islands at the same time.

Winston Churchill urged every effort should be made to destroy or dislodge the *Tirpitz.* On the 25th January he said.
"The destruction or even crippling of this ship is the greatest need at sea at present. No other target is comparable to it ..... the whole strategy of the war, turns at this period on this ship, which is holding four times the number of British capital ships paralysed, to say nothing of two American battleships retained in the Atlantic. I regard this matter of the highest urgency and importance."

The only arm capable of destroying her in her steep sided berth was Bomber Command. The first attack was made on the 29th January by 16 heavy bombers. It was not until the 12th November 1944, after many more attacks that 29 Lancaster bombers, led by Wing Commander Tait of "Dam Buster" fame finally made an end of her.

Far to the south, the channel dash was taking place. In a daring and well prepared operation, code named "Thunderbolt-Cerberus," the Brest Squadron sailed at 11 p.m. on the 11th February, and with massive air cover brushed past the British air and sea attempts to stop them. They would have reached the North Sea unhurt, had not both *Scharnhorst* and *Gneisnau* received severe damage from mines off the Dutch coast.

Strategically the channel dash was to our advantage. The concentration of enemy ships in northern waters, though a terrible threat to the Russian Convoys, made it easier to maintain a watch over them, while the threat in the Atlantic, particularly to those convoys bound for the Mediterranean, was immediately reduced. On the other hand it was a bitter blow to our naval pride.

Only a week after the channel dash, the Home Fleet was warned by intelligence that heavy German units might be at sea. On the 21st February our aircraft sighted both the *Admiral Scheer* and *Prinz Eugen* with a destroyer escort moving north; on the next day they were in a fiord near Bergen. Admiral Tovey's superior forces tried but failed to intercept them on their way to Trondheim, though the *Prinz Eugen* was badly damaged by a torpedo from the submarine *Trident,* just as she was entering this harbour to join up with the *Tirpitz.*

Thus menaced, the Russian Convoys had the full attention of the allied leaders. Both Stalin and Roosevelt urged more aid to Russia, and the pressure of the overall strategy forced Churchill to direct the efforts of the Home Fleet towards the Russian rather than the Atlantic convoys. Measures were taken to provide maximum protection from the enemy surface fleet in the area between Jan Mayen and Bear Islands, rather than east of there, where the U-boats and Luftwaffe were chiefly operating. Outward and inward convoys would in future be sailed so as to cross this area together under the protection of the Home Fleet; and air reconnaissance of Trondheim would be increased even further.

The continued loss of ships in the vicinity of the Kola inlet was of great concern to the Admiralty. To bring a convoy safely for 2,000 miles against the worst the enemy and weather could do, only to have ships sunk almost in sight of their destination was tragic. Rear Admiral Burroughs sailed to Murmansk in *Nigeria,* the flagship of our cruiser squadron. There he met and sought the co-operation of the Soviet authorities to provide anti-submarine sweeps and air cover for the final stage of the passage, when our crews were most tired and escorts short of fuel. He met with little success; later convoys were met by Russian destroyers, but no significant air support ever materialised. In the final reckoning, statistics were to show that 20% of our Arctic convoy losses had occurred in this last short leg of the journey.

The time had again come for *Trinidad* to leave the shelter of Hvalfiord and relieve the *Sheffield* from her stint on Patrol Black. On a cold grey morning, with a biting wind raging through the narrow rocky inlet trouble occurred: the capstan jammed. The anchor had to be hoisted somehow. Then and there a procedure was adopted that is seldom seen or used in any large ship; weighing the anchor by hand. The scene which unfolded was reminiscent of Nelson's day. A dozen long stout spars were inserted into slots in the capstan head, and a swifter (or rope) was passed round their outer ends to form a large wheel. Teams of 5 or 6 men to each spar pushed the capstan round, and by this primitive method the anchor was drawn to the surface one link at a time. In sailing ship days this was the only way and the backbreaking task was enlivened by a fiddler, playing lively tunes, standing on the top of the capstan; as much to keep the men in step as to cheer them up. The difference on this occasion was that in place of a fiddler, the Royal Marine Band installed itself rather precariously, on top of "A" turret and played sea shanties. The cold was so intense that one by one the instruments froze. As the last trombone spluttered to its untimely end a bandsman was heard to say, "Talk about cold, even me bloody spit's froze solid."

Sportingly, one of the violinists climbed on to the slowly rotating capstan head and we had the rare spectacle of "Fiddler on the Capstan." He played until his fingers too also froze, leaving the drummer still on the turret top and able to beat out a step. Nearby the crew of a United States warship gazed in astonishment at this very singular and historical performance.

The last few fathoms before the anchor was recovered seemed to provide increased difficulties. The reason was clear when it at last appeared above the surface. Dragging over the bottom it had picked up a heavy steel covered cable, which extended from the mainland and was now bar taut. Every possible effort was made to disengage the cable, but without success. Finally, one of the Shipwright Artificers had to be lowered over the side in a bosun's chair with an oxy-acetylene burner to cut it away. The authorities in Iceland were highly displeased by this action, even though this was hardly the occasion for seeking permission through the normal channels.

With this slow and cumbersome task completed, we were able to leave the security of the fiord and make our way out into the waters of Patrol Black. Three days later, proceeding south-east, we rendezvoused with a large minelayer and together made our way undetected towards the coast of Norway. For the next two days mines were laid in a position north-east of Asafiord near Trondheim, where only six weeks before the *Tirpitz* had taken refuge. A number of these mines broke adrift due to the atrocious weather; so our best marksmen were kept busy trying to explode these drifting hazards and the look-outs even busier, trying to spot them.

Our return took us through the fiords of the Faroe Islands, giving us a splendid opportunity to gaze on the breathtaking beauty of the scenery. As we made our way through the narrow waterways, the cliffs on either side rose sheer at first, then more gradually towards the summits of the tall mountains. Thousands of feet up, their snow covered peaks were stained coral pink by the reflected light from the crimson Arctic sunset. Across the waters we could see what looked like miniature houses, brightly coloured and lodged in tiny folds in the mountains. Drawing nearer it became clear these were normal houses lying at the feet of the mountains. It was only then that the true proportion and majesty of these towering peaks were fully revealed to us.

By the 3rd March, *Trinidad* had arrived at Scapa Flow once more; but all hope of even short leave was quickly dispelled by the news that we were to steam north, in the company of *Liverpool*, to collect our escort destroyers, *Fury*, *Echo* and *Punjabi*, before proceeding to a point south-east of Jan Mayen Island.

Tactical operations now moved rapidly into gear. Reports were received that the *Tirpitz* might move out with the object of intercepting the P.Q.12 convoy sailing outward bound from Iceland and the Q.P.8 convoy returning from the Kola inlet. Fully determined that the German forces should not only be contained but that they should be destroyed, Admiral Tovey sailed on the 4th March in his flagship *King George V*, in company with the aircraft carrier *Victorious* and six destroyers to join up with the battleships *Duke of York* and *Renown*, the cruiser *Kenya* and their escort.

Despite the British superiority in the total concentration of their forces, Admiral Tovey's difficulty lay in how to position them. Not only had he to find the enemy, which meant deploying his ships far afield, but he had to do so in groups having sufficient power to be certain of success once the enemy was found. The new German battleship alone was a formidable foe, she had eight 15-inch guns in addition to her powerful secondary armament. She carried six aircraft, 2,500 men, 12.6 inch armour and displaced over 42,000 tons, which was well in excess of any one unit under his own command.

At midday on the 5th March a Focke-Wulf Condor

reconnaissance aircraft sighted and reported P.Q.12's position and course. This news brought a decisive response from the German Naval Staff. Later on the 6th March one of our watching submarines, the *Sea Wolf* off Trondheim signalled that a battleship or a heavy cruiser was at sea: the former was correct. The *Tirpitz* under the command of Admiral Ciliax, together with three large Narvik class destroyers as escort, was out and heading north to intercept P.Q.12, unaware of or even in spite of the presence of the Home Fleet.

If only he could find her, Admiral Tovey was in reach of the opportunity of bringing the *Tirpitz* to action and destroying her. Unfavourable weather had again blanketed the area, making aerial reconnaissance impossible for either side.

At midday on the 7th the two convoys, amounting to 31 ships in all plus their escorts passed each other south of Bear Island. The *Tirpitz* had passed close to this point only three hours previously; while at noon the Home Fleet, believing the enemy to be south of the convoys, passed 60 miles to the south-west. The blind were seeking the blind. So it continued, the tracks of the British and the German forces crossed and re-crossed the convoy route as they searched for their quarries.

Previous to this Admiral Ciliax had detached his destroyers to make a sweep to the north, which resulted in one of them sinking the *Ijora*, a Russian straggler from Q.P.8. Twelve hours earlier he had been forced to release his escorts, which proceeded to Tromso to refuel. He then took the *Tirpitz* on a final sweep alone, first to the north then to the west until finally by early evening on the 8th he abandonned the search and turned south for the Lofoten Islands.

Trinidad and *Liverpool* were at that time heading north only 50 miles off the Norwegian coast. By the following day they were in a position off Jan Mayen island protecting the rear of the returning Q.P.8, which was heading south-west and clearing the danger area.

Admiral Tovey, like his opponent, also had had to send his destroyers off to refuel. He was heading south-west in the belief that *Tirpitz* had by now returned to Trondheim. But the monitoring of the German radio wave lengths and their tell-tale transmissions indicated to the Admiralty that she was still at sea and coming south. In the early hours of the 9th Tovey turned his fleet towards Norway and increased speed to intercept.

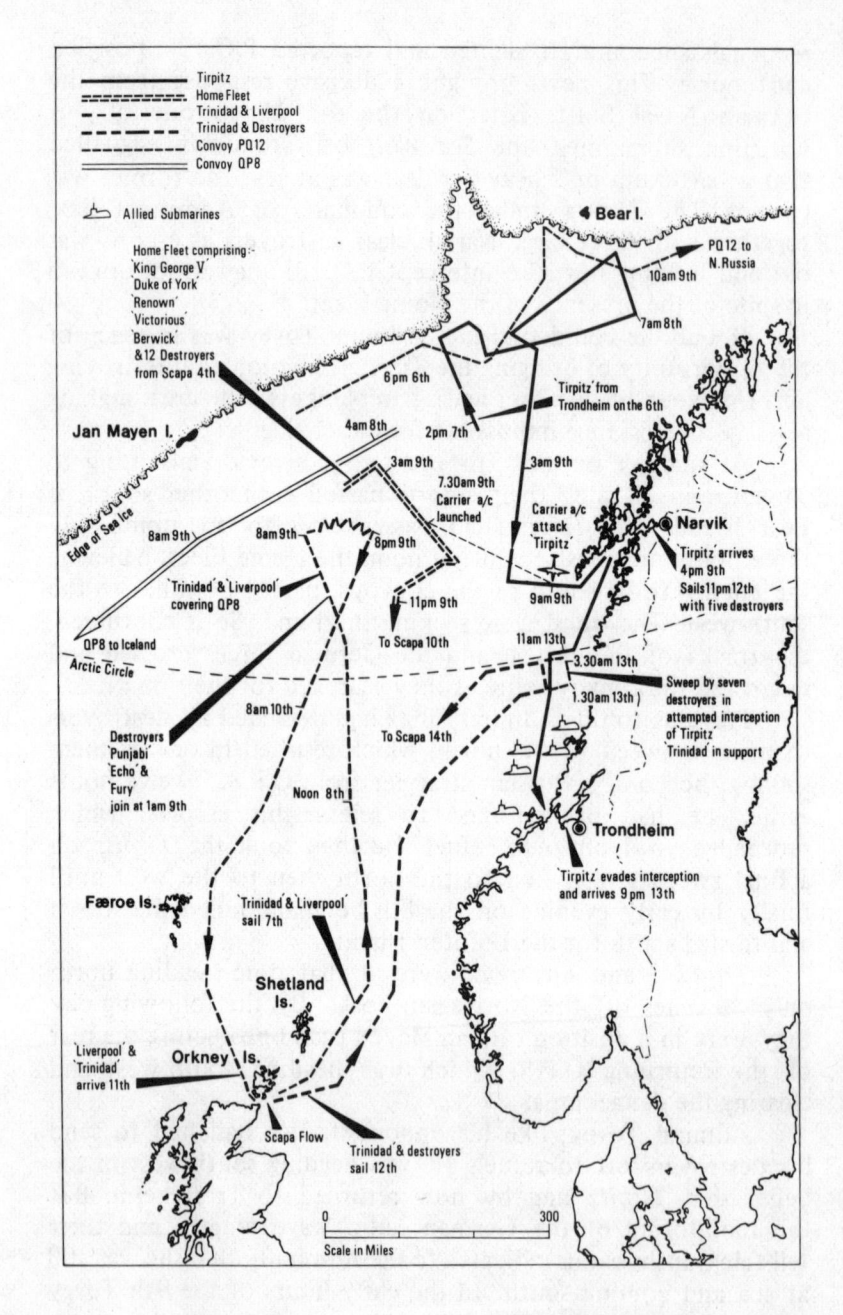

Fig: 2 Fleet movements 4th – 14th March 1942

Reconnaissance aircraft from the *Victorious* sighted the enemy battleship at 8 o'clock that morning, and a strike force of Albecore torpedo bombers from the carrier attacked her as she escaped towards Narvik through Vestfiord. Though surrounded by torpedo tracks she was untouched, whilst two of the British aircraft were lost and *Tirpitz* reached Narvik that afternoon.

We returned to Scapa Flow on the 11th March to find the Home Fleet already at anchor. After refuelling, *Trinidad* left the following morning in the direction of Norway. With us were 7 destroyers intent on an interception of the *Tirpitz*, which was travelling south down the coast towards us on her return to Trondheim. Once again atrocious weather conditions lowered visibility. Unknown to us, a reconnaissance plane flown off the *Tirpitz* to survey the area in advance of the battleship spotted us through a cloud break. This plane immediately signalled back the course and position of our task force, reporting that eight destroyers were proceeding north. *Trinidad* having been mistakenly identified as a destroyer.

During the early hours of the 13th, when in a position 90 miles north of Trondheim and only 20 miles from the coast, we made a concerted sweep across the possible course of the enemy ship. When this proved unsuccessful the search was abandoned. Three hours later the *Tirpitz*, the most powerful battleship in the world passed south-west through the same waters.

To the south again strategically placed, close to the mouth of Trondheim Fiord, were the allied submarines; the British *Trident* and *Sea Wolf,* the Free French *Junon* and the Norwegian *Uredd.* Forewarned, Admiral Ciliax with his escort of five destroyers avoided these forces with the help of the poor visibility. At 8 o'clock that evening the *Tirpitz* entered Trondheim. The hopes of the Home Fleet to bring her to action were never fulfilled, as there she stayed, a target for the R.A.F.

The following few days were calm enough to allow one of our two Walrus aircraft to be catapulted off on U-boat reconnaissance. None of us cared for this, as it later meant stopping the ship for long periods while craning the flying boat back on board again.

Imperial War Museum. *A shot of "Trinidad" from the Walrus plane.*

A shot of "Trinidad" from the Walrus plane

In the right atmospheric conditions and with a lot of effort, the Walrus could be coaxed up to 14,000 feet at a cruising speed of 100 mph with the full crew of Pilot, Observer and Air Gunner aboard. This was a rather gentlemanly if cumbersome looking machine. Unlike the Swordfish, the cockpit was reasonably well protected and one could even smoke in the front seats when airborne. A Lewis gun was mounted on the rear hatch just behind the propellor, and there was another hatch at the front, on which a second gun could be mounted if necessary. A trailing aerial was fitted which could be wound out of the aircraft after taking off, to improve radio performance. At the end of this aerial was a big bunch of lead weights and it was considered a serious crime to lose the weights, through forgetting to wind in the aerial before landing. Calculation of wind speed and direction involved a complicated routine. First a smoke float or flaming one at night was dropped — then the plane did two 180° turns timing the quarter and beam positions of the float. A mathematical formula allowed the Observer to calculate the wind speed, while a drawing exercise on the Bigsworth Board provided him with its direction.

Launching a Walrus was a complex operation. The catapult was located amidships, running across the cruiser from port to starboard. It was extendable by a further 10 feet either side giving a total run of about 45 feet. In the hangar the aircraft was kept on a trolly, which could be moved in and out by a system of wires under the deck, until it was on the catapult rails. It could then be wound out to the starting position. Here the engine was revved up and on a signal from the Pilot, the Catapult Officer fired a cordite charge, which shot the aircraft out over the sea, accelerating it from rest to 70 mph in the run available.

Former Leading Telegraphist Ron Bennet recalls that amongst his other duties was the operation of the direction finding apparatus when the Walrus was airborne. Sometimes he was not informed when it had returned and he then spent many hours listening intently for a missing aircraft that was safely secured in its hangar. It is better to draw a veil over his reaction when he finally correctly located the machine.

Landing again in the sea could be tricky, especially if it had started to blow up rough during the flight. Sometimes

Some of the crew of the Walrus plane.

The Walrus at Vaenga.

The Pilot and Observer.
Lt. "Jock" Thomson and S/Lt Paul House.

Top: Some of the crew of the Walrus **plane**
Bottom Left: The Pilot and Observer, Lt. **"Jock"** Thomson and S/Lt. Paul House
Bottom Right: The Walrus at Vaenga

they attempted to improve things by carrying out a "Slick" landing. The ship would execute a fairly wide turn across the wind and this gave smoother water for the plane to land on. In the bottom of the aircraft was a hatch, through which the camera was installed for taking vertical photographs. Unless the Observer checked that this was firmly closed before a sea landing, he would be reminded by a fountain of water at the moment of touch down. Once safely down the aircraft would then taxi alongside to be picked up. The aircraft had a four-bladed pusher propellor, which, though much better than the Sea Otter's tractor propellor in front, was still a forbidding sight to the member of the crew, who had to sit on top the centre section of the wing to hook on the Thompson Grab. Only when this had been mated correctly, could the crane hoist the aircraft out of the water and the cruiser get moving again.

On one occasion the Walrus returned from its flight and came to rest beside the ship as usual. The crane arm swung over with one of the lifting lines attached. But the line, not being secured correctly, dropped off the hook and fell directly on to the rotating propeller blades, entangling itself at once. Spray picked off the wave tops by the wind, further complicated matters by freezing the tangle into a solid mass. The Observer, Sub-Lieutenant House, crawled with some trepidation out on top and made a valiant, but unsuccessful attempt to cut through this snarl-up using a small hatchet. It was just then that the asdic operators made contact with an approaching submarine. It was far too dangerous for the cruiser to stay stopped any longer, so any further attempt to recover the Walrus was out of the question.

One can imagine the thoughts of the Pilot, Lieutenant Thomson and his crew, left in an immobilised plane as *Trinidad* disappeared over the horizon. It was an hour and a half before the relieved and thankful watchers saw *Trinidad* reappear to lift them back on board.

Operating flying boats from cruisers not only exposed the parent ship to great danger during recovery, but it became impossible under Arctic conditions. Worst of all it meant carrying hundreds of gallons of highly inflammable aviation spirit, which was a major fire hazard in action. Not long after this the practice was abandoned and the space saved was put to better use.

So far, the convoys to and from Murmansk had been largely successful. No losses had been sustained from P.Q.1, which had sailed in September 1941, until P.Q.8 – which we had escorted – suffered the total loss of the *Matabele,* but in terms of merchantmen only one had been damaged. P.Q.s 9, 10 and 11 had also been escorted through without loss, making a total of 103 loaded merchant vessels to reach Murmansk by the end of February. Although P.Q.12 and the returning Q.P.8 had avoided by the narrowest of margins an encounter with and almost certain annihilation by the *Tirpitz* and her escort, both convoys arrived safely at their destinations.

The sortie by the *Tirpitz* had failed to achieve anything except the consumption of oil fuel at the rate of 20 tons for every 10 miles steamed. The German war effort could scarcely afford to deplete its limited stocks of this precious commodity without more tangible returns. The disappointment of Admiral Raeder, the Commander in Chief German Naval Forces, was nothing to Hitler's rage at the amount of material that was still reaching Russia by this northern route.

Admiral Raeder realised how fortunate *Tirpitz* had been to escape the same fate as the *Bismark;* and blamed the lack of air support for what was nearly a disaster. He demanded that the strength of the Luftwaffe in Northern Norway be dramatically increased. Hitler agreed and the bases at Petsamo, Kirkenes, Banak, Bardufoss and Narvik, each with a sector of the convoy route to cover, began to receive massive reinforcements. This support together with a build up of U-boats in the Barents Sea, longer daylight and better flying weather was beginning to make the future of the Russian Convoys look extremely bleak.

The convoy P.Q.13, carrying a reputedly unlucky number, was likely to be the first to experience the full fury of an enemy determined to stop it; it was with some forebodings that preparations for its protection were begun. Even at this late date, our intelligence reported that the *Admiral Hipper* had sailed from Brunsbuttel on the 19th March and had slipped undetected into Trondheim on the 21st. Early the following day Admiral Tovey took the Home Fleet to sea, to provide cover for the threatened convoy.

5

P.Q.13 and the Great Gale

> *"These Arctic seas where men of war,*
> *Like playthings tossed,*
> *By waves shipped green from raging crests."*

At night on the 21st March *Trinidad*, re-fuelled again, sailed from Seydisfiord; but without the difficulties that marred her departure to escort the P.Q.8 convoy two months earlier. Above us the Aurora Borealis hung in the sky like crazily coloured curtains moving lazily beyond the dark sinister cliffs.

We were all very much aware that this time the conditions would be all in favour of the enemy. There would be no friendly perpetual darkness and whenever the weather was good enough we would have to beat off attacks from submerged and surface ships, as well as torpedo and dive bombers.

The rendezvous of *Trinidad* and P.Q.13 took place to the east of Iceland in the prolonged dawn of Sunday morning. A fleet of 19 ships, the most numerous yet, was deeply laden with tanks, lorries, aircraft and ammunition for the besieged Russians, who by now looked like being driven out of Europe. It was easy to see that these strategic cargoes were too menacing to the German plans to be allowed through. The escorting force provided, however, looked insufficient to complete the task that lay ahead. In close escort were two destroyers, *Fury* (Lieutenant Commander C. H. Campbell) and *Eclipse* (Lieutenant Commander E. Mack), with the small trawlers, *Blackfly* (Lieutenant A. P. Hughes, R.N.R.) and *Paynter* (Lieutenant R. H. Nossiter, R.N.V.R.). In addition there were three Norwegian whalers, *Silja, Sulla* and *Sumba*, being sent to Murmansk to act as minesweepers. The knowledge that the Home Fleet was at sea some hundreds of miles off — to provide surface cover against a breakout of The German Fleet — would have given little comfort to the ships' companies, even if they could have been told.

Nearly 2,000 miles away Q.P.9 sailed at the same time

as ourselves. This empty convoy also of 19 ships (Commodore, Captain H. D. Hudson, R.N.R.) had a successful voyage, uneventful except for the dramatic kill of *U.655,* which was brought to the surface by depth charges and rammed by the minesweeper *Sharpshooter.*

Gradually our convoy took up their stations under a sky flushed with red and orange hues. Agonisingly sluggish in their movements, they edged into lines to conform with the signals from the Commodore's ship, the *River Afton,* commanded by the distinguished merchant navy officer, Captain D. A. Casey, R.N.R. (later to receive the C.B.E., D.S.O., D.S.C. and R.D.)

In *Trinidad,* all hands off duty were called to Divine Service in the Canteen Space. When everyone was crammed in as best they could, Captain Saunders took the service and said a few words; the Chaplain, D. L. Graham, reading the lesson and announcing the hymns. As usual we finished by singing the hymn, "For those in peril on the sea." But on this occasion the words seemed to carry an even greater significance than they had ever done before. A little later, all hands heard the Captain broadcasting over the ship's loudspeakers, saying, "For the last few weeks we have been carrying out patrols, near and into enemy waters, but we now have to escort a convoy and a most important convoy through to Russia; running the gauntlet between Bear Island and North Cape, over which the enemy patrol with superior forces. We can almost certainly expect to meet their ships, U-boats and planes, and many of you will receive your baptism of fire — Good luck."

As we left the shelter of Iceland, we watched our recently adopted charges against a sky flushed with red and orange hues, as the sun rose in the dawn, soon to merge into a slow sunset. The coastline receded astern until it faded from view. Gone was the protection of the fiords, with their boom defences, and the feeling of security given by land close at hand. We were on our way. We were on our way individually, and on our own as a group of ships. We were committed by the allied governments to deliver the tools of war to those who were now taking the brunt of the Nazi aggression.

There could be no turning back, no matter what sort of punishment lay in store for the convoy. The tradition had been building up for so long, that no British seaman, naval or merchant, could be the first to consider retreat. The casualties might be high and the ships forced to part, but in time the survivors would arrive at their destination.

The convoy included ships of many nationalities and types. Identifying them by their flags, we could find ships from Sweden, Holland, Norway and America. They were big and little, old and new, dignified cargo liners, tankers with their volatile loads and rusty old tramps. All were essential — different in their appearance but with a common purpose. This at present seemed to be mainly trying to keep the same prescribed speed, while following a predetermined zig-zag course agreed at the convoy conference earlier.

Most of the vessels carried deck cargoes, piled high and chained down to withstand the inevitable heavy seas that would sweep across them. There was freight of every description: food, iron ore, medical supplies, guns, bombs, planes, machinery, trucks and tanks. A few, with nothing visible above decks, could well have been ammunition ships. There would be no need for lifeboats if a torpedo found its way into one of these.

Our admiration went out to the sheer guts of these merchant seamen. It was bad enough for us, but they had little or no defence against either air or submarine attacks. They had no speed except only that of the slowest, the most modern ship could only plod along like the oldest, a perfect target, a duck that must not fly. The smallest ship in the convoy was an old tramp, already known for her fluctuating performance. For the time being she had a full head of steam and came charging up through the line of ships, erupting volumes of black smoke, to the sound of ribald cheers as each one was passed. Two or three miles further on she almost predictably ran out of power, as if her clockwork motor needed winding up again. Once more the ships in the convoy overhauled her, but this time the cheers were to urge her on.

Convoys no longer proceeded in two long lines, bow to stern in line ahead. They spread themselves into several lines so that the fleet was often wider than it was long. In this formation ships were able to protect one another's flanks to some extent.

When the night turned into impenetrable darkness *Trinidad*, with her latest and most up to date radar installation, was able to search for, find and place the convoy just where it should have been in the ocean. But in the convoy itself, there were no such modern aids. Red-eyed look-outs and weary helmsmen peered into the inky blackness. No lights not even a torch could be shown. The responsibility of steering even a moderate sized ship blind in the middle of a fleet, grows from the initial strain into a mental torment, as one anticipates possibilities. Would one hit the stern of the ship ahead, which would not be seen until it was too late; or would one of the other vessels on a parallel course lose position and suddenly appear out of the dark right across ones bows.

The first early light of dawn found all the convoy still there, but somewhat dishevelled and untidy as the ships shuffled themselves back into station. All the while like a hen looking after a brood of chickens, *Trinidad* steamed around and ahead of the convoy. Her radar aerials continually searched for aircraft or ships, while a section of her gun crews was always closed up at stand-by action stations. The destroyers and smaller escort vessels kept closer contact with the merchant vessels, giving protection all round by searching the depths with their asdic gear. The word A.S.D.I.C. is made up of the initial letters of the Allied Submarine Detection Investigation Committee, which was set up after the First World War to see what could be done to lessen the submarine menace in the future. When this committee disbanded, Great Britain developed her own submarine detection equipment from the best ideas that emerged from these meetings. This was the system that employed the echoes of ultrasonic waves reflected from underwater surfaces, and was superior to the equipment of any other navy.

Progress was quiet and uneventful. There was a growing feeling of satisfaction and even optimism. Things were going well — almost too well until the elements took a hand. With little warning a raging Arctic gale struck with vicious intensity and the weather became a greater threat than the enemy.

> *This restless raging rolling sea,*
> *That squirms and turns and pits it's wits 'gainst rocks*
>   *and ships,*
> *And laughs at man's incompetence.*

The sea rose very quickly. Each enormous wave, marble flecked with translucent whiteness, reared itself up into an awesome mountain of water, sometimes as high as sixty feet, which then rushed down on to the ship as if to engulf her. Every time it seemed impossible that any man made structure could survive the impact of so great a mass of relentless green water. By comparison, deep in the trough between two of these great waves, the quiet seemed unbelievable. Then followed the long haul, climbing slowly up to another foam lashed crest — there to re-encounter the unbridled force of the tempest, tearing at everything and screaming like a thousand devils. Periodically a giant among the other waves would break and come roaring down over the fo'c'sle, wrenching off anything that was not bolted down or not an integral part of the structure. Heavy boats, high above the surface in davits and held in place by two gripes, were snatched away like toys. Guardrails were twisted and bent into grotesque shapes. Storage racks which had once supported rows of Carley floats were rifled and emptied except for odd floats, which were inexplicably spared. Even the large reel that housed the steel wire hawser used for towing another ship, weighing a ton and a half and fastened securely to the deck, was picked up like a cotton reel and catapulted through the air in a wide arc into the boiling sea.

On the bridge and other exposed positions, binoculars became useless as the windborne moisture froze on the lenses. The freezing spray froze into ice as soon as it came into contact with the steel decks and superstructure. This, supplemented by intermittent snowstorms, turned the cruiser into a power-propelled iceberg.

Men going on watch sometimes had to cross open stretches of deck to reach their stations. On one occasion Able Seaman Cooke making his way along the upper deck had a nightmare experience. He had just reached the safety rail placed alongside the torpedo tubes, when he turned and saw an avalanche of water pouring down towards him over the edge of the fo'c'sle deck. That moment he thought was to be his last. Flinging himself at the rail, he wrapped his arms and legs round the bar in a desperate attempt for survival. The deluge struck, tearing at him with all its power, but he was able to hang on until the dreadful ordeal was over. Other men caught by the sea were lifted and carried bodily aft until they crashed with a sickening thud against a turret or some other obstruction in their path.

Below decks and in the turrets, men who had been

thoroughly hardened to the normal heaving and lurching of the ship in a seaway, now became victims of seasickness all over again. These men had been closed up at stand-by action stations for what seemed days on end. Now they were utterly exhausted and numbed with cold. Some dozed standing up, others draped themselves across a gun barrel or whatever else would conveniently support them. There was a general state of mental inertia that came with the physical exhaustion, so that it became a major problem to sum up enough energy to carry out the most simple task. Chain smoking helped to steady frayed nerves and everywhere between decks the stale air, empty cartons and butt ends bore witness to this.

The conditions down below were chaotic. Anything that was not tied or screwed down found its way on to the deck, to join the mass of gash which shifted with every new movement of the ship. In the galley at the height of the storm, dinner plates, cups, saucers and cutlery all tumbled down in a deafening crash. Then, in spite of the fence around them, still simmering pots of soup and stew jumped off the hot stoves to spew their gooey contents all over the broken crockery and galley utensils. This happened when the cruiser had taken a monster wave beam on. Later the records showed that she had listed so far that another two degrees would have capsized her.

By the third day the gale had eased but not before it had already achieved what the German Navy could not accomplish throughout the war; the complete dispersal of a convoy. We were alone and our merchantmen were scattered over 150 miles of turbulent seas. The greatest chance of survival for any convoy under attack lies in its close formation and protecting screen of escorts. But now every ship was like a straggler, on its own, totally unprotected and an easy target for a U-boat without any chance of retaliation. The *Fury* and *Eclipse* were known to be about 60 miles astern rounding up what ships they could find. Someone broke radio silence and we received a call for help which the enemy would also have heard.

Slowly but surely the merchant ships discovered one another. Firstly forming groups of two or three, which then joined up with other little groups. Over the hours which immediately followed the storm, the convoy shepherded by the destroyers and armed trawlers developed into two separate flocks. One consisting of nine ships was four or five miles astern of us. It included the armed whaler *Sumba* and formed into three columns, was headed by the *Scottish American* as the Acting Commodore's ship. David Rollo, who was serving in this Royal Fleet Auxiliary bunkering vessel carrying petrol and oil fuel, has given this interesting description from the merchant sailor's point of view.

"After the big storm which scattered the convoy, we had time to check our damage. The flying bridge was completely washed away and all the life boats and rafts had disappeared. The crew's accommodation in the forward section was washed out in several feet of water which froze solid, resulting in the crew having to sleep in the engine room.

Soon after daybreak we found ourselves to be alone, except for one ship out on the horizon. This was a Dutchman who, seeing the Blue Ensign, tacked himself on behind. Gradually, the other waifs and strays found us and proceded to line up astern, full of very worried men — feeling very naked without any escort for protection and literally steaming past the enemy's doorstep. The armament in our ship, amounted to four very ancient Lewis guns, left over from the 1914 war and one even more ancient four-inch gun, which everyone was frightened to use in case it blew up. It was not long before a lone German aircraft flew over us and to our surprise made no attempt to attack. We soon realised that he had spotted a single ship on the horizon, trying to catch up — from the resulting explosion she must have been sunk. She was two-funnelled and I believe a Panamanian. A little later, another bomber flew in low to attack us with its bomb doors open wide, but the bombs themselves failed to drop. This sort of thing had been experienced by other ships and the probable explanation was that the bomb releasing mechanism had frozen. No-one can describe the relief felt by everyone when the destroyer *Eclipse* arrived."

The second group was some 70 miles eastward and ahead of us — it was made up of six ships, two of which lost contact as a result of later enemy action and fell astern.

Five of the stragglers found difficulty in rejoining any

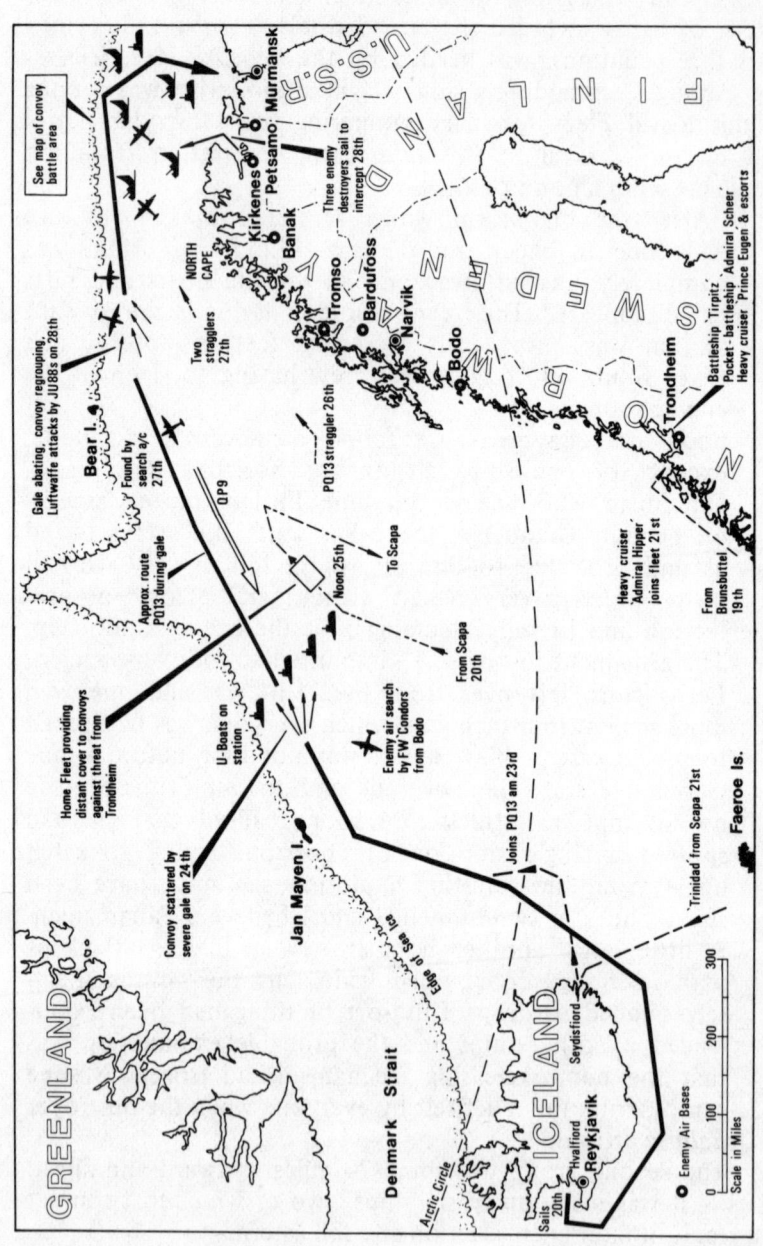

Fig: 3 Route of convoy P.Q.13 20th – 30th March 1942

group. The *River Afton* found herself near Narvik, right on the enemy's threshold; but in spite of this succeeded in arriving at the Kola inlet. Another two, *Empire Ranger* and *Raceland* steaming well ahead of the eastern group, were dive bombed and sunk. Later on the *Bateau* was also found and sunk by enemy destroyers. The remaining straggler, the *Harpalion,* finding herself dangerously close to the North Cape, went on ahead at all possible speed, in an effort to make the Kola inlet.

While this regrouping was going on, the *Trinidad's* radar operators were flashing on their sets for short bursts of only a few seconds at a time – in an effort to find as many ships as possible.

As expected it was not long before a Blohm and Voss reconnaissance plane discovered us and settled down to watch us, content to circle round us at a safe distance. The interception of its transmissions clearly indicated that we had been reported back to the enemy headquarters. Although it was hopeless we opened fire. The plane turned on seeing our gun flashes, and even made the signal, "Your shots are falling short." The gun crews named him "Snoopy Sam" knowing he would stay there until the ice barrier drove us further south towards the Norwegian coast.

Inevitably, a little later, the enemy bombers came in droves from the bases at Tromso, Banak, Bardufoss and Kirkenes. Inside the radar office excitement was growing with each new report and every few moments the operators would inform the bridge, "Aircraft on the Screen", "Two waves of aircraft approaching from the south," or just, "More aircraft". Simultaneously over the Action Broadcast System came the order, "Action stations – action, repel aircraft".

Hardly had this announcement died away, when the ship seemed to erupt into a crescendo of explosions as every gun that would bear engaged the dive bombers. After selecting their targets, the bombers came hurtling down through the low clouds to release their bombs before climbing back into the sky. The attacks went on for some hours, many of the aircraft concentrating on *Trinidad.* At one time there were six Junker 88's above us, three on the port quarter and three more screaming down on the starboard beam, some of the bombs missing us by as little as 20 feet. There can be nothing but praise for our gun crews who continued to serve their guns in the face of this terrifying form of attack. If it had not been for their efforts, the enemy pilots would have been able to aim with greater accuracy and we should have been hit again and again.

So we should not be like an "Aunt Sally" at a country fair, Captain Saunders was also taking avoiding action using the maximum speed and manoeuverability of the cruiser to dodge each attack, and then making a dash for the nearest patch of poor visibility at top revolutions. During the attack, Lieutenant Commander Herepath, the Air Defence Officer, gave a running commentary over the broadcast system, so that those between decks could have some idea of what was going on up top. Despite the dramatic nature of attack at such close quarters, his voice stayed firm and quiet. To those who could not see the action, he was great.

The attacks halted by the end of the day. One merchant ship had been sunk for the loss of two enemy aircraft. In spite of the weight of bombs aimed at her, *Trinidad* was undamaged except for her radio installation. During the action the Central Communications Office had experienced great difficulty in transmitting signals to inform the Admiralty that we were under bomb attack and what our position was. One near miss on the port side had shaken up the main W/T transmitters, and all the valves and lamps in the central circuits were disintegrated internally; even though they were supported in what were called shock proof mountings. The emergency transmitter on the bridge took over and one of the escorting destroyers relayed the messages to Admiralty, using *Trinidad's* call sign. Chief Petty Officer Telegraphist Dale and Petty Officer Telegraphists Blanket and Treen between them did a fine job in maintaining W/T communications throughout the engagement, most of the time under direct enemy air attack.

By midnight on the 28th, we received a signal from the Senior British Naval Officer North Russia, to tell us that a Russian submarine had reported three enemy destroyers heading north-west towards the remnants of the convoy. They had come out of their base at Kirkenes, having been given our position and course by the Luftwaffe. They then had had considerable luck as they picked up one of our stragglers, which they immediately sank and whose crew revealed details of the constitution of our convoy and the warships protecting it.

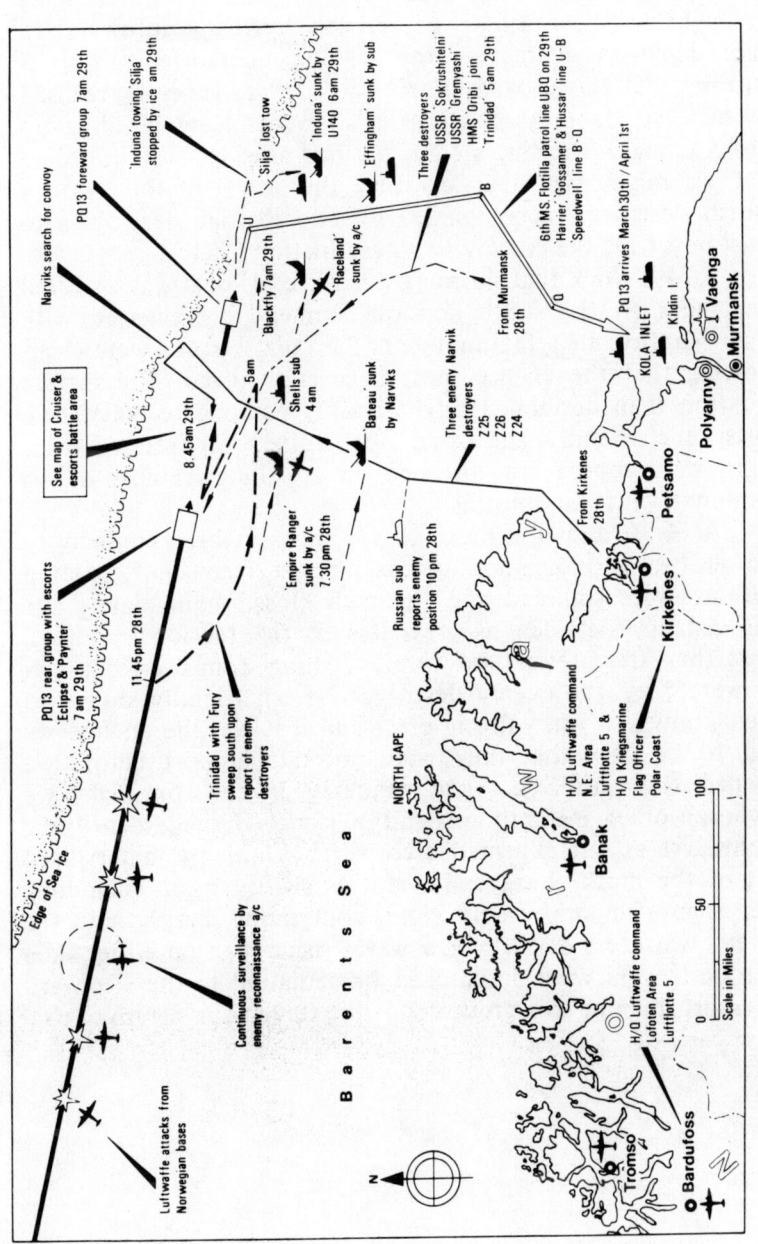

Fig. 4 Convoy P.Q.13 Battle area

Trinidad at once collected *Fury* and made a sweep during the night to the south to cover both convoy groups; and to place *Fury* in charge of the leading unescorted group if required: but this proved unnecessary. It was generally realised by men at stand-by positions that events were building up into a climax. The ship's company had already been informed that we might expect at any time the arrival of the *Oribi*, a British destroyer, accompanied by two Russian destroyers to assist in getting the convoy to its destination safely.

At 4 o'clock that morning a surfaced U-boat was detected two miles to the south and was immediately engaged with heavy gunfire. In a few moments the radar screens were clear, showing that the enemy must have crash dived. The surface situation then developed into a doubly complicated one. Two units, one friendly the other not, both comprised of three ships, were approaching through the appalling visibility of fog combined with snow storms.

At 6.30 a.m. the radar screen showed three contacts to the eastward, indicating approaching surface craft. Action stations were sounded and the men closed immediately. As the distance between us grew less so the tension mounted. Were they the support we were expecting from the Kola inlet or were they the enemy destroyers? Even friendly ships had been known to open fire in error and if it was the enemy, we had to be sure that they were not our support before we opened fire ourselves. Then suddenly in the dim light we saw each other, instantly recognition signals flashed, identifying themselves as our expected escorts. They quickly materialised out of the murk ahead and swept as swiftly past. Their long grey shapes uncomfortably close, contrasting sharply with the silvery whiteness of their bow waves rising high on either side. The destroyers were despatched immediately to the westward to escort the nine ship group following three miles astern of us.

6

Trinidad Torpedoes Herself

The position of the convoy and its escort relative to *Trinidad* and *Fury* can be summarised as follows:- Three miles astern were *Scottish American, Tobruk, El Estero, Gallant Fox, Empire Cowper, Normadora, New Westminster City* and *Eldora*, with the Norwegian whaler *Sumbra*. Providing the screen for this group were the Russian destroyers *Sokrushitelni* and *Gremyashi*, the British destroyers *Eclipse* and *Oribi*, plus the armed trawler, *Paynter*. Approximately sixty miles ahead the *Empire Starlight, Mann, Induna, Effingham, Ballot* and *Dunboyne* only had the tiny *Silja* for their escort, and some 20 miles further to the south-west the armed trawler, *Blackfly*.

The three German destroyers, having swept the area to the north-east without success, turned south-west towards the convoy route, so that without being aware of it, the two forces were heading directly towards each other. Heavy black snow clouds were drifting at sea level, further decreasing visibility which was already poor.

In the radar office the duty operator, Able Seaman Jack Anderson was the first to see an echo on the screen, followed by two more approaching rapidly on the port bow. He immediately reported the range and bearing to both the bridge and the transmitting station. On the bridge it was clear from the tension in the operator's voice that he knew he was on to something, as indeed we realised he must be. With the whereabouts of our own ships and Russian escorts already known, there could be no doubt that this was the enemy.

For many, as the Captain had foretold, this action would be their first confrontation with the German Navy, and their baptism of fire. Nor would this be any remote impersonal engagement, firing at an unseen enemy ten or fifteen miles away. As our combined speeds gave a closing rate of 45 knots, it was clear that in a matter of minutes we should be looking down each others gun barrels. On the bridge and look-out positions, all eyes strained to catch the first glimpse of the

German destroyers through the snow filled gloom. In every turret the crews stood beside their guns, tense and pale, watching the faces of the telephone operators, through whom would come the order from the Transmitting Station to open fire.

A sea battle demands a different sort of courage from those whose action stations are deep down below and are unable to see the enemy. They have to operate in an atmosphere of suspense, prepared for catastrophe, but praying it will pass them by. At any instant the ship's side might disintegrate inwards, with icy water or fire finishing the deadly work of the explosion. For both sides this conflict was inevitable; not to destroy was to be destroyed. We were up against the might of a dictator whose lust for power had plunged the world into war. Ordinary men were facing death or mutilation so that those who survived could one day resume normal life again.

At 8.45 a.m. A.B. Harper, in the adjoining radar office, found the range of the echoes to be 10,000 yards, three minutes later 6,000 and at 8.50 a.m. it had dropped to 4,000 yards. Up 'till now the British warships had an advantage over the enemy, as the Germans had not as yet realised the full potential of radar for detection, and were only using it to establish ranges for gunnery, while we were using it to plot their exact position. As the seconds dragged past and the range decreased further, the tension mounted. Until identification was established Captain Saunders was withholding the order to fire.

Far down near the bottom of the ship was the Transmitting Station, where the complex gunnery predictions were calculated and relayed to the armament. The twenty one man crew of this compartment was busy plotting the enemy's changing position, having little time to engage in any conversation other than a terse, "Well this is it boys – Good Luck!" The complement of this station was made up of the Officer in Charge, Warrant Gunner Nat Gould, two Ordnance Artificers, two Seamen, one Writer, a Supply Petty Officer and 14 Royal Marine Bandsmen. The musical duties of these bandsmen, though already put to good use in the ship, were secondary to their main assignment, which was the skilled operation of a highly technical computer controlling the main armament and anti-aircraft guns.

The function of the Transmitting Station was, as it is in other Royal Naval ships, to receive from the radar office and elsewhere such information as range and bearing of the target. Then to calculate, amongst other things, what its course and speed was compared to ours. This then had to be converted into training and elevation angles to aim the guns. Even the temperature of the air could alter the flight of the shells, and this and other ballistic information had to be allowed for.

Once the computer had evaluated all this data, the directions were relayed to the guns, constantly bringing them up to date in step with the changing situation. These directions took the form of pointers moving on dials and once the guns were brought into line with these, bells from the Transmitting Station confirmed that the armament was on target and triggers could be pressed. The efficiency of the system was largely dependent upon the precision with which the men in the Transmitting Station processed the constantly altering information coming into them.

The location of this vital link in the armament control was calculated to give the maximum degree of protection to both the computer and its crew. It was placed below an armour plated deck and in many ships surrounded by store compartments filled with sacks of flour and other dry provisions. In *Trinidad,* being built to a tonnage limitation, the Transmitting Station was enclosed on either side by oil fuel tanks. The knowledge of this did not contribute to the sense of well-being felt by the occupants of this cell-like space.

Now in the final moments before the impending action the dramatic impact of the occasion acted as a stimulant. Fear was forgotten with the realisation that the defence and safety of the ship and her crew might depend upon how quickly and accurately they could make their calculations, and as the enemy sped closer the turrets received the new training and elevation directions.

Suddenly, with the unpredictability typical of this Arctic climate, the visibility cleared and there immediately ahead, at less than two miles and closing fast, were three of Germany's big Narvik class destroyers, carrying guns almost equal in calibre and fire power to our own cruiser. These were units of the German 8th Destroyer Flotilla, or Zerstörer-Flotille Narvik; and later identified as *Z.26, Z.25* and *Z.24.* They were large vessels in comparison with the British destroyers, having a complement of 320, a displacement of 2,600 tons, and, it was said, could reach a top speed of 38 knots.

Still closing at speed, they appeared to be slightly in echelon from line ahead and at a range of only 3,000 yards or just over 1½ miles. Leading Signalman Jordan had only made the first two letters of the challenge when, without further hesitation the Captain gave the order to open fire, almost synchronising this with the hoisting of the stirring signal "Enemy in sight" — so often seen in practice exercises, but never before in earnest.

Then all hell broke loose.

Anything that could be fired through a tube fired. The main six-inch armament, the four-inch anti-aircraft guns, the pom-poms and even the machine guns blazed out destruction. We had caught them unready, and the curtain of fire hurtling from our main armament crashed into the leading destroyer setting her on fire. Our shells could be seen exploding amidships creating considerable flame and smoke, stretching between the mainmast and the after funnel.

Inside the forward and after gun turrets, the Royal Marines and other gunnery rates, went to war. They gave a near faultless display of gunnery. The raw crews, despite the hurried training and earlier despair of the Gunnery Officer, had risen to the occasion like veterans.

No more fumbling or misjudgment, each shell was rammed home with precision, each long sleeve of cordite was slipped dexterously into its chamber before the breech slammed shut; followed immediately by the roar of exploding propellant as the gun fired and recoiled. The acrid smell of cordite fumes belched back into the turret as the breeches were flung open, and seemed to galvanise the men into machine like efficiency, — "Load and fire," — "Load and fire", the orders came faster and faster — it was their lives or ours.

The Germans, recovering from their surprise and the ferocity of our assault, began to return our fire and two shells smashed into *Trinidad's* port side aft, just under "Y" turret. Here damage control parties had been lying on the deck as instructed, to minimise casualties; all except one man, a Leading Stoker who was standing in the middle of a compartment near to "Y" barbette. He laughed at everyone and told them how ridiculous they all looked. Suddenly there was a terrific crash as the shell entered through the ship's side accompanied by the searing heat flash as it exploded. For a time all was confusion, water was gushing out of a fractured fire-main. A high pressure air line burst with an alarming roar and a fire started in one of the cabins. Then when the ship turned she listed over to port and sea rushed in through the shell hole. For a few minutes there was minor panic and everyone made for the ladders.

However, reason quickly prevailed and the damage control party set to work to make first aid repairs. The fire was extinguished and eventually lighting was restored with a temporary system. The shell had made a hole some five feet square just above the waterline. There was one casualty however: lying on the deck was the Leading Stoker with the lower part of his body shattered and bleeding terribly. He died in great pain calling a woman's name.

The repair party repaired the fire-main and air line before turning their attention to the shell hole. The acrid fumes of the enemy shells were being augmented by the smoke from our own rapid salvoes of the six-inch turret directly above them. As they struggled to plug the hole with a patchwork of hammocks, the men's faces were being scorched by the muzzle flashes of our own guns. Something was needed to hold the hammocks in place, and the nearest object of sufficient substance was the door of the Captain's cabin. This stoutly constructed mahogany slab was wrenched off and was soon shored up against the temporary plug. Later there were some hard questions about that door, but it had saved the situation, because the sea washing over the hammocks quite quickly froze them into a solid mass — like blood clotting over a wound, making the patch almost watertight.

Relentlessly *Trinidad's* salvoes crashed into and around the leading German ship. In desperation her Captain, Commander George Ritter broke off the engagement and swung his ship to starboard, heading north-west into some thick snow clouds.

With the leading destroyer out of the action, the Director Control was ordered to shift target to the second destroyer. Here again the shells found their target with devastating accuracy, shattering her after turrets. Nevertheless, three modern destroyers deployed at such a close range, firing from different sectors and with 24 torpedoes still unused put *Trinidad* in very great danger. In anticipation of a torpedo attack, Captain Saunders ordered the wheel hard to starboard, which turned his ship away from the enemy. This shrewd move meant the ship now presented the minimum target to the enemy, yet allowed "X" and "Y" turrets to continue firing at the two remaining enemy destroyers.

Everyone could feel the cruiser heeling right over shuddering from stem to stern as she turned at full speed. With the turn two torpedo tracks were clearly seen as they passed close to the port side, quite harmlessly due to this timely and violent alteration of course. After holding this bearing, directly away from the enemy and parallel to the torpedo tracks for two or three minutes, *Trinidad* again swung hard to starboard. This completed a triangular course, so that she was now heading due north at a speed of 26 knots in order to remake contact with the enemy. Although the three German destroyers now had the cover of a snow storm, the decreasing visibility had also caused the second and third ships to lose contact with their damaged leader, *Z.26*.

On *Trinidad's* bridge the sleet and snow had again made the use of binoculars almost impossible — a much clearer view was being obtained by the naked eye. So, although nothing could be seen from the bridge, the radio direction finder obtained a contact at 8,000 yards. This could only be the enemy, so engine revolutions for 30 knots were ordered immediately. 15 minutes later we were overhauling him with the range down to two miles over to starboard, still unseen, but proceeding on a parallel course to our own.

Captain Saunders now decided to alter course towards the enemy, in order to engage him while passing obliquely across his stern. Within a few minutes both the bridge and the look-outs clearly saw black smoke in the haze, and almost immediately after that, the shape of the enemy ship from which the smoke was billowing out in clouds. With the range now down to a little over a mile, *Trinidad* opened fire with "A" and "B" turrets and utterly destroyed the enemy's three after gun mountings. With the range still decreasing the enemy zig-zagged desperately to escape further damage. *Trinidad* manoeuvered into a position away to starboard to bring the after turrets to bear as well. This also allowed the port four-inch and close range weapons to open up, in an effort to drive

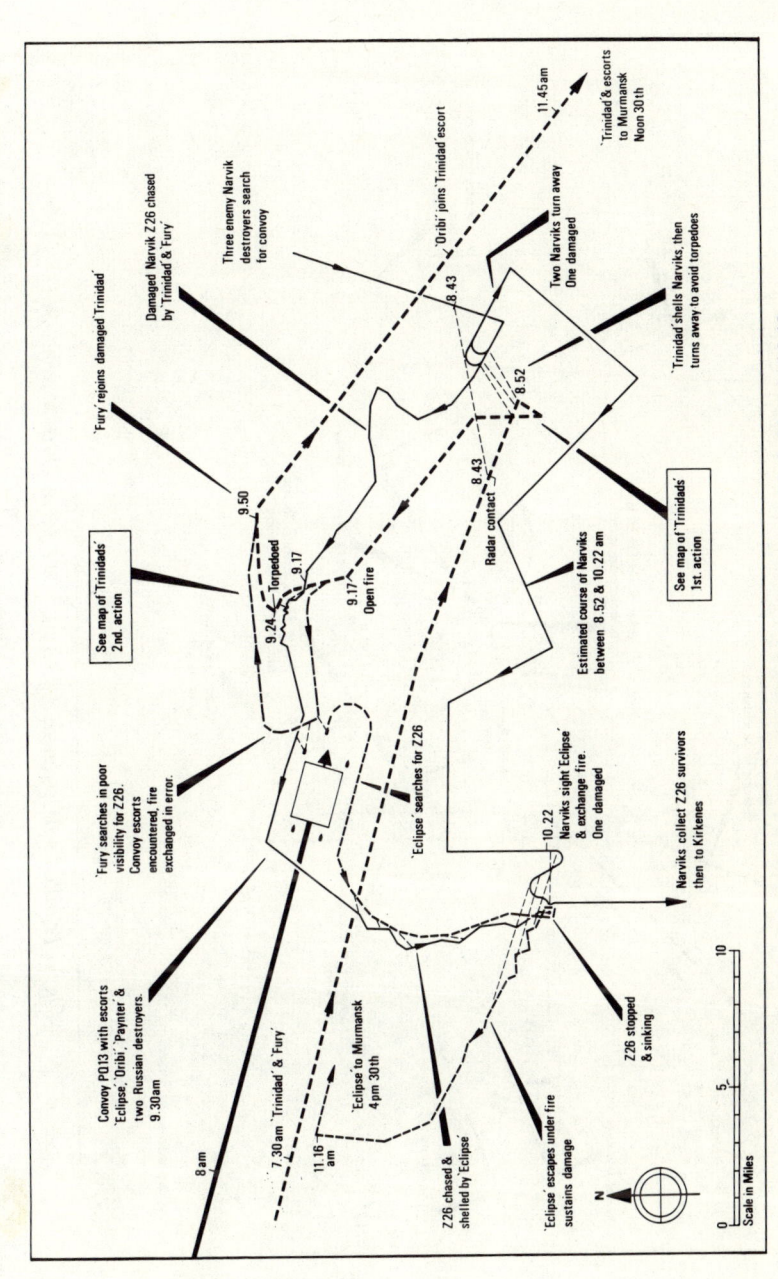

Fig: 5 Cruiser and escorts Battle area – a.m. 29th March 1942

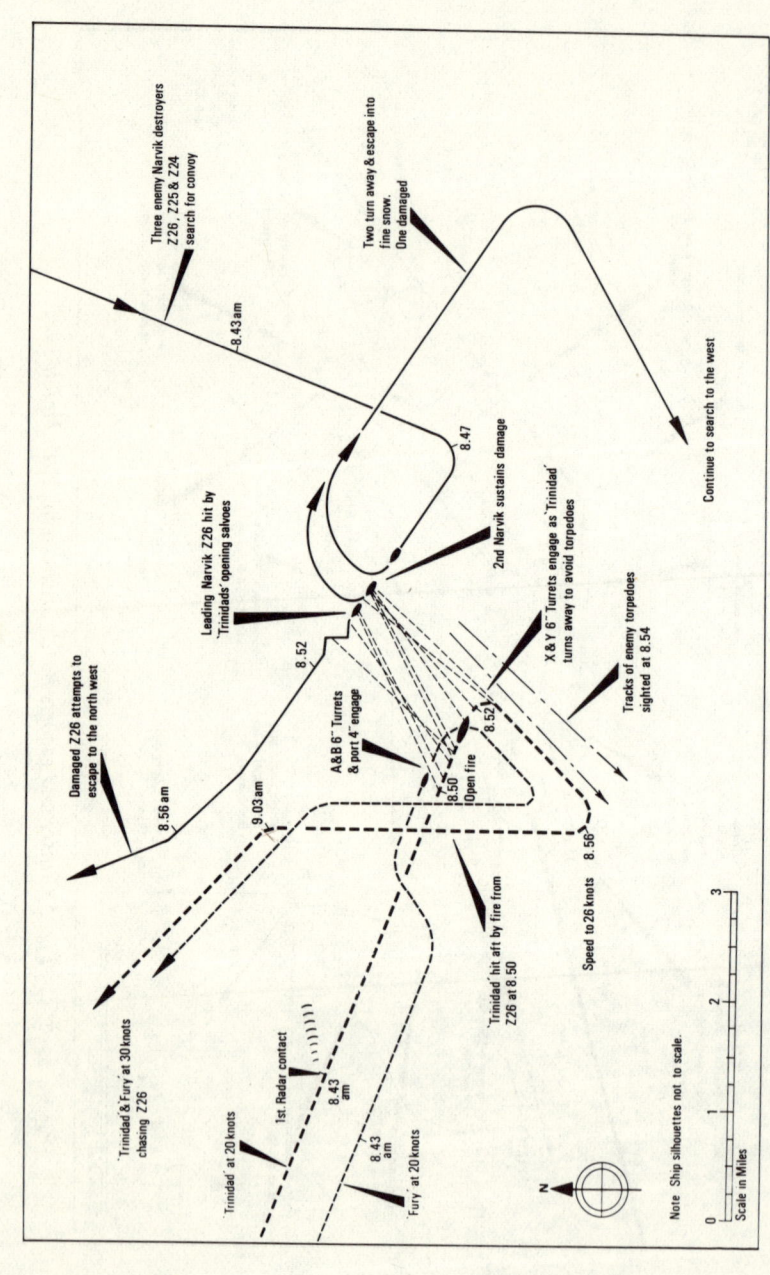

Fig: 6 *Trinidad's first action 8.43 a.m. – 9.03 a.m. 29th March 1942*

the German crews away from their torpedo tubes. Three more direct hits were registered just below the destroyer's bridge, but still defiant, her Commander swung his ship to starboard in order to get his forward turret to bear. Only one salvo was fired and that ineffectually, apparently due to the punishment already received.

The manoeuvre to engage the enemy across the stern had three tactical advantages. It allowed all *Trinidad's* turrets to dominate the target. It prevented the German from using any of his eight 21" torpedo tubes from either side and reduced his opportunities of using his forward turret. Once again Captain Saunders had established and maintained a tactical superiority.

As the chase continued, we passed close to numbers of German sailors supported by their life-jackets in the sea, many of them already dead. These men had presumably been either blown overboard by the force of explosions or had jumped to avoid being blown up.

If the convoy was to be protected, there was only one course of action open to us; dispatch the enemy as quickly as possible, then swing round to the south-west to seek out and engage the other two enemy ships. If either or both those destroyers should meet up with the oncoming convoy, now not far distant, they would lose no time in sending as many merchantmen to the bottom as possible, subject to what defence the convoy's escorts could provide.

It seemed incredible that the *Z.26* could have suffered so much damage without sinking or blowing up. Just before 9.30 a.m., to finish her the Torpedo Officer Lt. Cdr. Dent, fired one torpedo from *Trinidad* when the enemy was well on the port beam. Holding his fire with the other two for a few seconds, until the target angle improved, he fired again. Neither of these last two torpedoes left their tubes owing to some deficiency in the anti-freeze compound allowing them to have frozen solid in the mounting.

Minutes later, some 200 yards away on the port beam, a torpedo travelling directly towards us broke surface. Although the wheel was put hard over it was impossible to avoid it. The British tradition of not dramatising situations was upheld by Captain Saunders, who looking over the top of the bridge parapet quietly observed, "It looks remarkably like one of ours".

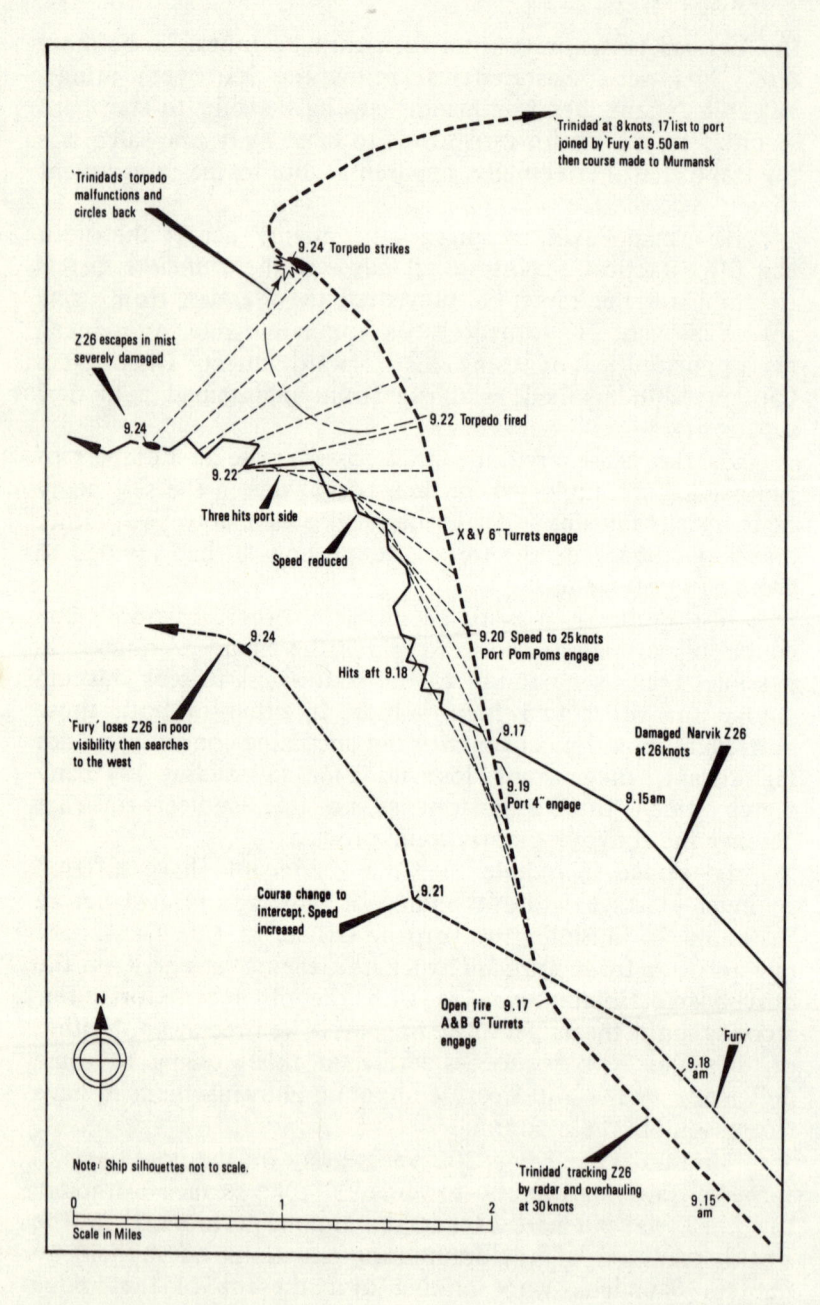

Fig: 7 Trinidad's second action 9.15 a.m. – 9.24 a.m. 29th March 1942

Inconceivably the gyro-mechanism controlling the course had jammed and the torpedo had run amuck. It had the whole Arctic Ocean in which to run wild, yet it had swung round and taken a course to intercept the ship — steaming at full speed — which had fired it in the first place. With this menace threatening to reverse the whole course of the action, officers and men watched helpless. The lethal steel fish rapidly closed, struck the port side just forward of the bridge and exploded, tearing away a huge section of the ship's side.

The disaster was as unique as it was unpredictable. The probability of this happening must be less than one in a million. Yet fate had wrenched success from our grasp and given us this bitter wound instead. At the later enquiry, a frozen gyro was the opinion of the experts and was the official and only explanation for the disastrous behaviour of the torpedo. But soon after the action, an alternative solution was put forward by one of the executive officers, who was stationed in the Air Defence Control position and had watched the whole episode. While the torpedo from *Trinidad* was speeding on its way towards the enemy ship, a salvo of shells from our six-inch turrets fell short of the stern of the German destroyer and immediately in the path of the torpedo. It was his view that the turbulent wall of water thrown up by the exploding shells threw the torpedo completely off its course and changed its direction back towards us.

Whatever the explanation might have been, the explosion which occurred momentarily lifted the ship and a huge column of black oily water rose into the air, covering everybody on the compass platform and look-out positions on the port side. The torpedo had exploded in the Royal Marines Barracks, flooding the forward Boiler Room, destroying the forward Damage Control Headquarters and killing instantly numbers of officers and ratings in these spaces.

Two decks below in the Transmitting Station the explosion had created more devastation than was at first appreciated. The compartment had been plunged into darkness at once, then as the ventilation system drew fumes from the seat of the explosion down below, the conditions became most alarming. What was not known, however, was that the bulkheads surrounding them had been critically weakened and were barely able to support the tremendous pressure being exerted on them by thousands of gallons of oil fuel on the other side. As soon as the supplementary lighting had been switched on, the crew of the Transmitting Station took up their positions round the computer tables and set about trying to re-establish communications with the bridge.

The long compartment was divided into a small and a large section. The small one dealt with the high angle gunnery and the larger with surface gunnery. In the high angle section, Corporal Roger Palmer found that his computer table had been split right across and was useless. Neither here or in the larger section, could any contact be made with the bridge. Reporting to the Officer in Charge he shouted, "I am out of communication with the bridge." Nat Gould replied, "You had better come in here". Right away Palmer walked through with a seaman and two Bandsmen until they were standing by the main computer table, which was immediately adjacent to the foot of the ladder leading to the access hatch. Addressing the seaman, Nat Gould said, "Go to Damage Control and tell them we need assistance".

Reaching the top of the ladder, the seaman undid the clips and pushed back the heavy armoured hatch, only to be swamped by a deluge of oil and water which came pouring down through the opening. Clearly the decks above were being flooded with oil from ruptured tanks. Climbing a steel runged ladder and squeezing through a small hatch in a listing ship is difficult enough; but to have to do so with the rungs running with slimy black fuel oil is almost impossible. However the seaman was through in a few seconds.

Nat Gould, realising that in a very short time they could all be trapped decided to evacuate the compartment. With great courage and dignity he stepped back, placed his hands on the holding bar of the table and said, "Abandon T.S. — It is every man for himself". The scramble up the ladder became a struggle for survival. Roger Palmer managed to pull himself up the ladder and through the hatch opening, followed by two other Bandsmen, Lew Barber and George Lloyd. By the time Lloyd reached the ladder the oil was up to his waist. It was a feat which would have challenged the strongest men, but whatever the physical ability of these three men might have been, it was more than made up by their will to survive. Gasping

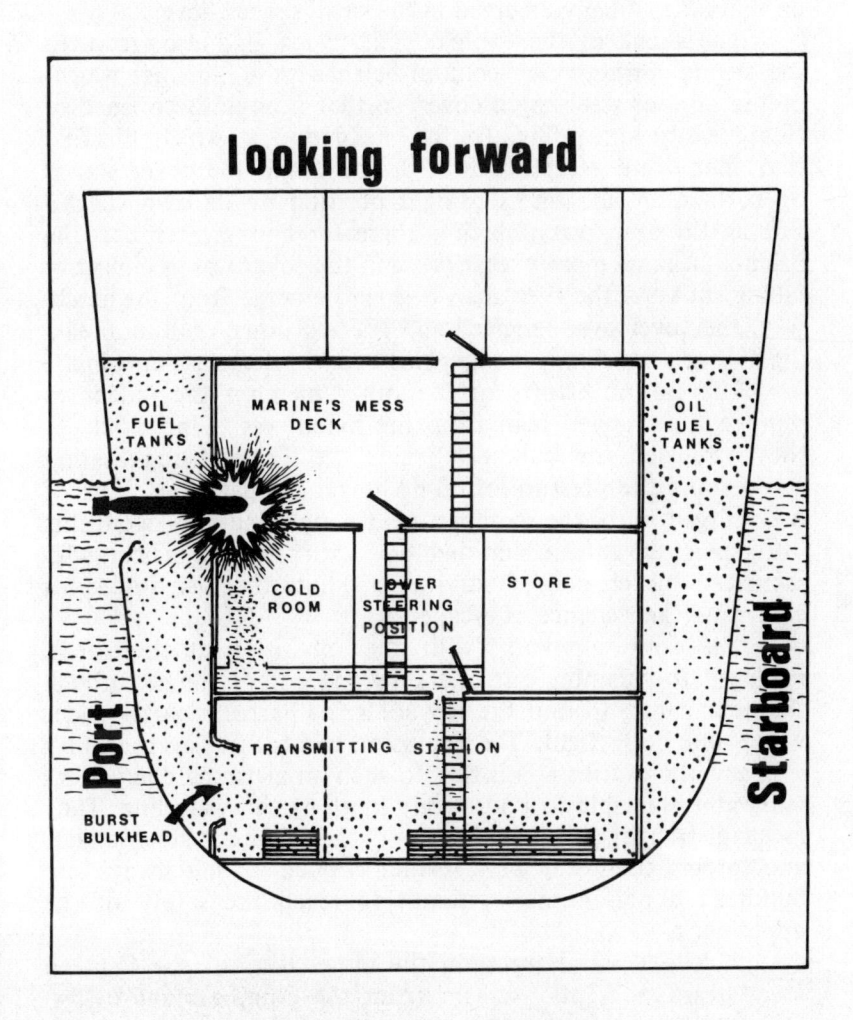

Fig: 8 Position of torpedo impact.

and spluttering from the cascade of oily water pouring down on them they finally emerged in the small space above.

The shock of the explosion, it seems, had also fractured the strong spring which counter-balanced the immense weight of the armour steel hatch cover, so that it could be opened or closed easily and safely. During the period in which the first four men were escaping through the hatch the cover stayed open, held in an almost upright position by its own weight. But as flooding was inducing a greater and greater list, the balance became more precarious and the cover was in danger of falling shut. As the fifth man began to emerge from the hatchway, the cover over-balanced and crashed down on him, breaking his back and firmly wedging his body in the small opening.

The frantic efforts of the other men on the ladder to remove the trapped man from the hatch was of no avail. As they struggled the bulkhead inside the Transmitting Station could stand the pressure of oil no longer and gave way. Tons of fuel surged into the compartment, engulfing the occupants in seconds. Seventeen men died and with them an officer, who sacrificed his chance of survival to allow the men under his command their chance of escape.

The four survivors, with the oil rising at their feet, managed to scramble out of the second compartment through the next hatch, to find the Royal Marine Barracks partly under water and in daylight. The explosion had torn away the ship's side and the cruiser was listing to such an alarming degree that sea water was able to pour freely in along the waterline. They raced distraught through the messdecks, climbing steel ladders and forcing their way past further clipped up hatchways and bulkhead doors in their attempt to reach the safety of the upper deck.

Able Seaman Harper on the upper level of the Canteen Flat, heard a frantic scream from the compartment below, followed in a very short time by one of these survivors, who came racing up the ladder saturated in oil. His appearance alone was frightening enough, but, when Harper and another crew member rushed over to help him, he, in his demented state imagining that they were trying to stop him from reaching the upper deck, tore at them in a frenzy with the strength of a maniac. For some minutes this fight went on, until eventually, a well delivered blow knocked him unconscious. By this time a number of other ratings had arrived and, while Harper and his shipmate recovered, they carried the unconscious man off to the Sick Bay.

An hour or so later, the three surviving Bandsmen met in one of the upper flat spaces. George Lloyd was still being violently sick from the after effects of shock, and Lew Barber just sat, dazed and unseeing. Roger Palmer turned to him and asked, "Where are the rest of the Band?" and was told, "They are no more Roger. There is only you, George and me left now". The loss of their comrades had made a deep and lasting impact on the four survivors. The Band had worked together as a closely knit unit for over twelve months, and prior to joining *Trinidad* had travelled regularly every Sunday from their quarters at Heybrook Camp near Plymouth to play in the morning service at Wembury Church. A memorial plaque to the Bandsmen who were killed, was later erected in the Church.

In the forward Boiler Room the damage had been just as severe. Following the explosion a wave of water swept through the boiler room carrying Chief Stoker Ellicott and his men to the foot of the escape ladder, where Ellicott and Stoker Petty Officer Oakley were badly burned by escaping steam. In darkness, waist deep in water and with the piercing scream of escaping steam all around them, it was a terrifying experience – until eventually the exit hatch was opened and they could make their escape from the rising flood.

Trinidad now lying stopped, began to take on an alarming list to port, with the sea flooding freely into the ship through her damaged side. At the moment of the explosion the port torpedo tube mounting had been torn out of the deck. The instantaneous listing, coupled with a great wave coming inboard at the same time, carried the whole fixture over the side. Torpedoman Bowditch, who was in the control seat of this set of tubes, undoubtedly owed his life to his own instinctive action and split second timing; for as the mounting started to move, he sprang for the rungs of a ladder and hung on grimly till the danger was over.

The *Fury* who had kept in close company with *Trinidad* during this action and had seen the torpedo hit, went on to chase the enemy. She soon lost contact due to the atrocious weather conditions. Then, some 15 minutes later a two funnelled destroyer was seen from *Fury's* bridge, straight ahead and approaching through the dim light. One of *Fury's* forward mountings opened fire, getting off two salvoes before the target was identified as the *Eclipse*. Fortunately no damage was done, and *Fury* turned about to rejoin *Trinidad* and give her any assistance possible.

The cruiser was now lying over to 20° with seas coming over the upper deck on the damaged side. A smaller hole on the starboard side, some ten feet square, had also been created by the torpedo explosion. One of the marines had been blown clear through this hole into the sea, but had been carried back again to the ship's side, where he had clung on to a trailing rope. As the ship had listed further and further over to port, he had been able to pull himself up the starboard side on to the upper deck; and was the only man to be saved from that messdeck.

The scene on deck was quite unreal; men walked casually around the upper deck or calmly stood waiting with a resigned attitude for whatever might happen next. Around us was the freezing sea, in which no man could survive longer than a few minutes. Below decks was the carnage of dead and dying men and the steady ingress of water. Not far off and slowly plodding in our direction appeared the rearmost group of the convoy.

David Rollo in the leading merchant vessel, *Scottish American,* relates how the situation appeared to him.

"At the time of *Trinidad's* action we were in a snowsquall with extremely poor visibility and had just finished breakfast when action stations sounded. We closed up at our massive armament (the aforementioned machine guns) and it was sometime before we realised that the whining sound we heard in the distance were in fact shells and not bombs as we expected. When we came out of the snow storm later we were appalled to see *Trinidad* dead in the water listing heavily to port with smoke and steam belching out of her starboard side. Here was a brand new cruiser put out of action and possibly sinking — what chance would we have with our pop guns?"

All *Trinidad's* Carley Floats were now out of action, as they had become entirely iced up so that no amount of hacking with ice picks and hatchets would move them. With the ship heeling and the decks covered in ice and fuel oil, it needed both strength and dexterity to progress even a few yards. The gun crews of the port four-inch mountings, wrapped as they were in cumbersome arctic clothing and wearing sea boots, found movement particularly difficult. These men having been on the deck directly above the torpedo hit, were dazed and shocked by the blast. Lieutenant John Daniels Royal Marines, had difficulties in getting them to understand the urgent need to throw overboard some of the heavy amunition from the lower side. Just then a figure covered from head to foot in oil came up on deck and asked if he could help. He had just escaped from a compartment adjacent to the Transmitting Station and was quite unrecognisable. It was only later he was identified as Midshipman Graham Mann, who after the war was to become the Duke of Edinburgh's sailing master and subsequently skipper of the yacht *Sceptre,* in a bid to regain the "America's Cup".

In the attempt to correct the list, parties of men on the instruction of officers were trying to throw overboard anything moveable from the port side, that could not be dragged up to the higher side. Even one of the Walrus aircraft, which had been badly damaged was pushed over the side. Some of the radar ratings were out on deck trying to help, but were unsuitably dressed for outdoor work in the Barents Sea. Men who normally work in radar offices, where the valves in the sets give off a great deal of heat, do not wear many clothes; and some of the working party only had a sheepskin vest and a pair of trousers on.

From the bridge came a call over the loudspeakers for all portable heating apparatus, such as electric fires, to be taken to the temporary sick-bay to bring some sort of comfort to the badly shocked and wounded. Next a double tot of rum was ordered to be taken by all hands, and this was a life-saver for many. Frostbite was beginning to take its toll and it was weeks before those who suffered it, fully regained the use of the afflicted limbs again. One of the officers accompanied by the Chaplain, came up to one of the groups standing awaiting developments on the upper deck, and said, "I don't want to put the wind up you chaps, but I think you ought to know, I give the strongest man alive only three minutes in the water — you see what I have done", and then tapped his deflated life-belt. The Chaplain smiled and wished them luck.

Below decks every attempt was being made to reduce the

list to port. Starboard compartments were being intentionally flooded with sea water and oil fuel pumped overboard from the port tanks. Then came some good news, we were holding. Those below were working wonders. Thanks to the efforts of the Damage Control parties the increasing list had been checked. Given time, the optimistic forecast was that it could be reduced.

A large merchant ship continuously steamed close alongside, with ropes, ladders, knotted sheets and anything else that could be hung over the side to save a life should we have to jump for it. Captain Saunders repeatedly asked her Captain to look after himself, but he kept coming back through the gloom, steaming slowly past and asking how we were.

Many of the wounded had been rescued by this time, and the most critical cases brought into the wardroom and screened off. When the rum was issued, the Master-at-Arms asked the ship's doctor if he thought any of these men could take their ration. The doctor agreed to this, adding that some were in such a hopeless condition he doubted if it would make any difference either way. One rating, who was in this state, nodded eagerly when asked if he would like a little rum. The Master-at-Arms raised him gently to allow the liquid to pass into his mouth and a little later he asked for a cigarette. This when lit and placed between his lips, was followed by two long and contented draws, but a moment later his head lolled sideways and he slipped quietly out of this life.

With *Trinidad* critically damaged, virtually helpless and wallowing in a rising sea; it was the escorts turn to become involved in the engagement with the German destroyers. The badly damaged *Z.26* had turned south from her escape course northward and was making for home water. Inadvertently she passed very close to the convoy and was sighted for a moment by the *Sokrushitelni*. The Russian destroyer quickly opened fire on the German before she disappeared again without returning a shot. A highly complex and potentially dangerous situation developed, with Russian, German and British destroyers catching brief glimpses of each other as they passed and re-passed often firing at each other. It was here that the incident involving *Fury* and *Eclipse* occurred.

A few minutes later, with the convoy adequately screened by the two Russian warships on each bow, and the British destroyer *Oribi* guarding the rear, Lt. Cdr. Mack in *Eclipse* decided it would be safe to rejoin *Trinidad*.

Able Seaman Jennings, a gunnery rate in *Eclipse*, says that when the signal was received from *Trinidad* that she was engaging the enemy, had badly damaged a destroyer and was after another, some apprehension was felt. But this turned into alarm, when a few minutes later a second signal was received reporting that she had been torpedoed. Their hearts sank, as they realised that it was now up to them and the other escorts to defend the convoy against the bigger guns of the predatory German destroyers. This particular ship was not only much smaller than her opponents but carried only two 4.7-inch guns forward, one of which was completely iced up and could not be used.

Sweeping around to the south, *Eclipse* almost at once picked up a radar contact at two miles, and closed thinking it might be a stray merchant ship. She cautiously approached with her one and only forward gun loaded and ready to fire. This was certainly not a merchant vessel. Through the murk the vague outline indicated a warship, and the impression given at first by the big gap between the funnels was that this could be the *Trinidad*. However a small reddish ensign flying from a stay and a clearer look on approaching, showed her to be one of the German destroyers. The vessel flashed a recognition signal, perhaps assuming the *Eclipse* to be one of her own consorts. All doubts were then dispelled when the Leading Signalman on the bridge shouted, "German Ensign Sir."

They had come right up into 500 yards range of the stern of the badly damaged *Z.26*. Without further ado the *Eclipse* opened fire with her forward gun. The German destroyer's speed had not been impaired and without attempting to fire back, she tried to escape into the mist. If at this moment the *Z.26* still had had her after guns operational, she could have blown the *Eclipse* to pieces. But instead it could be clearly seen that the three after turrets of the enemy were completely demolished as a result of *Trinidad's* earlier shelling. One gun was cocked up into the air, another hung crazily over the side while the third seemed to be locked on to the port beam position, pointing down towards the sea.

The British ship, hard on the German's heels, took up the chase and soon began to overhaul. The German Captain made desperate efforts to bring his ship around to get his forward guns to bear, but Lieutenant Commander Mack was a match for him, nor was he to be denied his victory. Skilfully anticipating every move he clung tenaciously to the astern position however much the enemy twisted and turned. He could not afford to make a single mistake, as given the chance the more powerful guns of his adversary would quickly shatter his smaller ship. Contact was almost lost on several occasions, when severe snow storms brought the visibility down to a few yards; but oil fuel leaks from the pursued ship left a trail which could be followed.

The *Eclipse's* 4.7 inch gun now began to find the target, and shell after shell slammed into the fleeing destroyer, but the conditions were almost impossible for the gun's crew. As *Eclipse* raced on through the blizzard, her own high speed forced the cold sea spray to come pluming up over the bow. This then fell in a freezing downpour on an all around the forward gun mounting and its crew. Unlike their German counterparts the British crews did not have the shelter and protection of a steel turret encasing them. They were out in the open, where any scrap of flesh left exposed would be flayed raw by the icy water. The gunlayers had to aim with smarting eyes peering through frozen eyelids as they strained to the utmost to stay on target. Loading numbers had to force their numbed hands and frost-bitten fingers to grasp the shells, which first had to be kicked free of the shrouds of ice that bound them to the ready use racks. *Eclipse* was now very low on fuel and this made her sensitive and liable to pitch and roll much more than usual. She listed excessively each time the wheel had to be put over to counter the enemy's avoiding actions. The men's feet on the ice covered decks would then slide from under them, thus further hampering the passage of the heavy ammunition into the ever hungry breech.

The German sailors could now be seen jumping overboard to avoid piecemeal destruction by the exploding British shells, even though their fate was even more certain once they were in the water. As pitiful as their plight might seem, it is as well to remember the scores of merchant seamen who had gone the same way in earlier convoys, and the many more who would do so, until the enemy was defeated. And there were the 198 men of the *Matabele*, who had been killed in these same waters as a result of an attack by German naval forces. Lt. Cdr. Mack had no alternative but to make certain that the *Z.26* was eliminated.

One shell from *Eclipse* hitting the enemy aft must have penetrated through into one of the cordite magazines; for there was a powerful explosion. The German destroyer still did not reduce speed. Some minutes later she suffered another direct hit on the starboard side. This one must have found and exploded in a boiler room, for at last the vessel rapidly slowed down and finally stopped.

Eclipse approached with care. The stern of the *Z.26* was now awash, with the after turrets and decks a complete shambles. Gradually the British ship moved up along the starboard side. The oerlikon and machine gun crews, tense as gun-fighters, waited ready for the slightest sign of retaliation. The big destroyer was however like a ghost ship, there was no sign of life and she was slowly sinking. Lieutenant Commander Mack swung the bows of his ship across the enemy's and came down her port side, giving the order "Torpedo ready," in preparation for the 'Coup de Grace'.

Suddenly two shells came screaming out of the sky, one falling just astern and the other some two hundred yards ahead. Once again that day, fate had turned the tables. Quite undetected, the two sister ships of *Z.26* were approaching at speed through the scattered snow clouds, firing with their main armament as they came.

The snow storms were unfortunately abating and the visibility improving; so, deciding that conditions were far from right for his ship to tackle the two larger ships, Lieutenant Commander Mack made off at maximum speed. His remaining torpedo was left unfired in case there was a chance of using it on his new opponents. With shells falling all around her and zig-zagging wildly, *Eclipse's* after gun was able to score one direct hit on the second German vessel. She herself received two direct hits, with splinters from several near misses holing her above the water line. The two shells exploding aft ignited some cordite charges and this caused heavy casualties among the ammunition handling parties. The *Eclipse* sped on, with the nearest group of snow clouds apparently getting no closer, and it was not until 20 minutes later that she reached the comparative shelter and safety they offered.

It is sobering to consider what might have happened if

the two German destroyers had persevered with their pursuit and battery of the damaged *Eclipse*. However valiantly the British destroyer would have fought to a finish, she would inevitably have been overwhelmed. Nor would *Fury* have been a better match for two of these big heavily gunned warships. This would have left the sorely damaged *Trinidad*, listing dangerously and rolling wildly in the big seas that were running. Unable to defend herself or escape, she would have been an easy target for a torpedo. Then taking their time the Germans could have eliminated the two groups of merchant ships, one by one, regardless of what protection the three remaining small destroyers could afford. The whole P.Q.13 convoy would have had to be written off as a naval disaster.

It might be just as idle to speculate what might have happened if *Trinidad* had not fallen foul of her own rogue torpedo. However, old sailors have always found a fascination in refighting old battles, even though this can never bring lost comrades back to life again. The cruiser could have collected *Fury, Eclipse* and *Oribi* and together, they could have quickly disposed of the two other German vessels. This would have created a considerable if temporary set-back for Hitler's northern naval forces, and many more merchant ships would have got through to Russia in the following months.

It should be remembered that *Trinidad's* prime role was to protect the convoy and, in the words of her sailing orders, to ensure, ".. its safe and timely arrival." To have taken the destroyers away at the outset in an attempt to bring the German destroyers to a decisive action, would have left her convoy exposed to attack from U-boats and from the air. It can be truthfully argued that in driving off the enemy ships from the convoy, the *Trinidad* had fulfilled her duty.

Eclipse now only had 40 tons of oil fuel remaining. After signalling her intentions to *Trinidad*, she set off independently on a course for Murmansk. Below and above decks, the situation although by no means critical was far from pleasant. Enemy shells had holed her sides extensively, carried away aerials and blown part of the funnel away. One rating had been killed and a tiny sick-bay was having to look after a dozen seriously wounded men. Owing to the exposure they had experienced together with the long hours spent closed up at action stations, most of the crew were by now in a state of exhaustion. Watches were relieved, new crews took over and double tots of rum were handed out. The *Eclipse* had had enough war for one day.

It was just at that brief instant of anticipated relaxation that the snow storm lifted momentarily and clearly visible on her port bow was a large U-boat on the surface less than 400 yards away. On top of this, as the two enemies recognised the other as an opponent, Lieutenant Commander Mack saw the wakes of two torpedoes converging on him. With the helm hard over, alarm bells ringing and action stations sounding once again, the *Eclipse* managed to swing away in time to allow the two long silver shapes to pass close but harmlessly by and disappear astern.

Carrying on round to port to commence a run in for a depth charge attack, he could see the U-boat was beginning to crash dive. With the *Eclipse* working up to full speed and the U-boat so close, Lieutenant Commander Mack had very little time to make decisions and even less time in which to execute them. For the commander of the U-boat speed and time were to be made allies if he was to escape destruction. Speed to get clear and time to lose his pursuer. For the captain of the destroyer speed and time were to be made his allies if he was to make a kill. Speed to catch the U-boat near enough the surface to ram her, and time to give his gun crews an opportunity to acquire and score hits on the target, before it disappeared. Equally important the men on the racks needed time, to set the depth charges to explode at the right depths.

But time was not on the side of the destroyer. She was not quick enough to catch the U-boat at the surface. When she arrived where the submarine had been only a few moments earlier, the only evidence of her existence were the swirls and eddies of a record crash dive. Down below the enemy was escaping and although *Eclipse* dropped pattern after pattern of depth charges, there was nothing to indicate that they had caused any damage. With even less fuel than ever and with his crew's endurance even further taxed, Lieutenant Commander Mack abandoned the hunt and once again headed for the Kola inlet.

7

Trinidad is Saved

Meanwhile optimism was rising every hour in the *Trinidad*. Down below the damage control parties were performing something only a little short of miracles. The fires in the Royal Marines Barracks had gradually been brought under control. The small arms magazine immediately below this messdeck had been successfully flooded to remove the danger of it blowing up from the heat generated by the fire above.

Just as this operation was reaching its final stages, a second fire broke out in the Torpedomen's Messdeck caused by hammocks and clothing igniting. The blaze was intensified by the oil on top of the flood water, giving rise to volumes of black smoke and heat. The Sick Bay above was gravely affected so that water had to be played on the deck to keep it cool. As several attempts to extinguish the fire on this messdeck proved to be unsuccessful, the whole area was sealed off and the fire allowed to burn itself out slowly.

Here, as in many other parts of the ship, the lack of lighting was creating enormous difficulties. Both primary and secondary electrical installations had been put out of action; and only a few places, the Sick Bay fortunately being one of them, were not in darkness.

The Supply Officer, Commander Harold, had one main concern and that was to reorganise the feeding of the ship's company as quickly as possible. He was handicapped by the fact that the galleys had been put out of action due to lack of electricity — which ruled out hot meals. Action messing was still in force, but in the extremely cold weather conditions the absence of hot meals was a dismal prospect, and, he knew, in the long run bad for morale. Right aft there was a small galley with a coal fired range, which was lit and set to work making relays of hot cocoa throughout the night. With over 600 men to satisfy the sluggish output of this small range was less than adequate.

Due to a comprehensive programme of pumping and

counter flooding, the cruiser was decreasing her list, bit by bit. Even so, this was no time for rejoicing; she was still lying well over, deep in the water, lurching with every sea, quite helpless and a perfect target for any enemy U-boat or surface vessel who might chance to see her. The remaining Boiler Room was hard put to provide enough steam to keep steerage way on the ship. This was only four knots, which was hardly enough to set course for the Russian Coast, now about 150 miles to the south-east.

The appearance of a long low grey shape materialising out of the mist brought an anxious moment. This was followed by a flood of relief and a round of cheers when she was identified as our escort *Fury*, returned from her brush with the enemy and near collision with *Eclipse*.

More help was on the way from the Kola inlet, as *Harrier*, *Speedwell*, *Hussar* and *Gossamer*, units of the 6th Minesweeper Flotilla, came to our rescue. *Harrier* set a course to find and escort us back to the inlet — leaving the others to round up the scattered convoy. While on this duty *Hussar* and *Gossamer* both sighted a U-boat, which quickly submerged on their approach. An hour later *Gossamer* obtained an asdic contact and both ships carried out concentrated depth charge attacks, and from all accounts it seemed probable that the U-boat was destroyed.

In the machinery spaces below *Trinidad's* decks, artificers and stokers were making every possible effort to increase the speed of the engines, but their partial success was only spasmodic. At least we were on our way — although not at the speed we would have chosen — only as fast as a man taking a walk. We had to get what comfort we could from the fact that we were moving towards the refuge of the Kola inlet.

The *Trinidad* was having other difficulties that had arisen as a result of her torpedoing. The explosion had wrecked the lower steering position, flooding the compartment so that it had to be abandoned. The ship had to be steered instead from the after steering position, which was directly above the rudder itself. Communications with the bridge had also been destroyed. The only way these could be re-established quickly was by organising a line of men stretching from the compass platform on the bridge, down to the steering wheel right aft, and passing the helm orders by word of mouth. Slow and cumbersome though it was, it worked, and ensured that we were going in the right direction.

Some time later the promised assistance started arriving. First in the form of the destroyer *Oribi,* and soon after the armed minesweeper *Harrier.* Her arrival had been delayed by a barrier of pack ice coming between us, and forcing her to make a long detour to avoid this obstruction. It was a comforting sight to see *Fury* and *Oribi* moving around us to maintain a continuous anti-submarine screen, with *Harrier* taking station ahead.

The U-boats had been converging all the while on the approaches to the Kola inlet, with the intention of intercepting any shipping making for the safety of this Russian port. Early that afternoon, out on the port bow, the *Fury* sighted a surfaced submarine about 500 yards from her. Bearing down on the enemy at top speed, the destroyer Captain tried to ram her, but without success as the U-boat was able to crash dive in time. The asdic contact was so strong however that no time was lost in developing a depth charge attack. Repeated patterns of these were dropped until the enemy, later identified as the *U.585,* had been destroyed. This success of *Fury's,* coupled to another of *Sharpshooter,* who at the same time had sunk a U-boat in defence of the returning Q.P.9 convoy, was particularly encouraging. It broke the run, prior to this, when no U-boats had been sunk on Russian Convoys.

Ships in the main body of our convoy were struggling onwards as best they could, but were in no condition to keep close station. Some were suffering from the effects of near bomb misses in the earlier attacks. Others were listing because their cargoes had shifted in the great storm, and the badly bombed *Harpalion* was following up a long way astern. The crews of these merchant vessels had already done a magnificent job just bringing their ships as far as this. They still had one more obstacle to overcome before they would be able to rest in the shelter of a protected harbour. Somehow they had to get past the ambush the U-boats had been setting.

The *Effingham,* a few miles ahead in the forward group, took the first torpedo, which, exploding in her Boiler Room, sunk this vessel in minutes. Even though some of her company were able to reach a boat, only a few of them survived the dreadful weather conditions.

Trinidad, though now well protected, was still in difficulties.

Although the light was now fading, the weather was growing worse. The wind was from the north and this was rolling up nasty seas, which she was taking on her port after quarter. At her slow speed of only four knots, this caused her to yaw from port to starboard and steer a most erratic course. Within an hour it was dark — even if the U-boats could hear us, at least they could not see us. But by midnight, such was the fickle nature of the climate in these latitudes, the wind had dropped, the clouds had dispersed and, as a quiet calm took the place of unruly seas, out came the moon. Not just a thin new moon, but a large round full moon, which lit up the ocean far better than the sun had done on the previous day. Aided by the Northern Lights, all was bright and clear with excellent visibility.

Dreamy love-sick poets, along with U-boat skippers, might well have eulogised on the possibilities of this beautiful and well lit night. But the appearance of the moon on this particular occasion generated far from romantic attitudes in the hearts and minds of us in the cruiser. However forceful and unprintable the phrases that were used to describe our feelings might have been, they could not do justice to the probability that even now *Trinidad's* black silhouette set in a silver sea was framed in the periscope of an enemy submarine. It was then that the engines stopped.

For some time salt water had been finding its way into the very pure water used to feed the boilers. Once this salt had reached a dangerous level, the boilers had to be shut down to prevent more serious damage all round. Within a few minutes the cruiser drifted to a complete standstill. The Engine Room staff, fully alive to the dangers of the situation, worked like demons to clear the trouble. A most eerie silence followed the shutting down of the forced ventilation fans. Like in a bad dream, there was an air of unreality hanging over the scene. Men stood around on the upper deck and talked in whispers. Each one of us was acutely aware that everyone else's spine was as chilled as one's own. There were only two sounds to be heard; the gentle lapping of the water against the ship's side and the occasional thud or clang from down below, as the Engine Room Artificers strove to get the ship moving again.

In the offing our three escorts worked like gun-dogs searching for game, repeatedly circling and back-tracking to warn off any predatory U-boats. Every second seemed a minute and these took an eternity to make an hour. Just aft of the hangar deck an old timer with grey hair, certain that this would be the end, sat calmly whittling down a piece of wood to form a bung. This he was going to fit into the hole of a large empty oil drum, in the hope that it would keep him afloat until he was picked up. He chose to ignore what he must well have known, that the temperature of the water was his most deadly foe.

At last the repairs were done and the propellor shafts began to turn again. We were on our way, but still at slow speed. While *Trinidad* laboriously made her way through the night, it seemed that the escorts were making asdic contacts with submarines. We could hear the detonations of depth charges going off, loud and clear, as attacks were made on the U-boats that were manoeuvering to finish us off.

As the night passed, the light of dawn came steadily to find us still moving south. Once more the weather changed, deteriorating until the wind quickly gathered itself into gale force. Again large seas were bearing down on the stern of the slow moving cruiser and played havoc with all attempts to steer a steady course. Just before 8 o'clock that morning she 'broached to'. The seas had finally forced the stern right round until the ship lay broadside on to the weather. In this vulnerable position the ship could well be swamped and lost.

In desperation Captain Saunders signalled the *Harrier* to turn back and attempt to get a hawser across our stern and pull us back on course again. But, by the time *Harrier* had rigged a tow wire and got into a position to pass it, *Trinidad* had got herself out of this predicament and was continuing on her course unaided. By now the Kola inlet was only 12 miles away. Two hours later we had 5 miles to go and, by noon, we finally and with great thankfulness arrived at our destination. We came to anchor opposite Rosta and without any delay started negotiations and preparations to enter the Russian dry dock which was there.

During these last few miles the Torpedo Officer, Lieutenant Commander Dent, had the watch on the bridge and noticed a small repeater indicator still illuminated on the compass platform. This told him that the generator in the Low Power Room must still be running. This seemed to be impossible, because the Low Power Room was below the Royal Marine's

95

Imperial War Museum *Ammunition ship exploding*

Imperial War Museum *Inside the Kola inlet*

Top: Ammunition ship exploding
Bottom: Inside the Kola inlet

Barracks, where the torpedo had exploded, and this messdeck was still under several feet of water. Up till then it had been logical to assume that all the compartments under this messdeck were open to the sea and flooded. But the evidence that the generator was still running, showed that this assumption was incorrect and there was a possibility that someone might still be alive down there.

Almost simultaneously with this discovery, the Warrant Shipwright, Mr. Tew, and Chief Petty Officer Share were carrying out an assessment of the extent of the damage below. While crossing over the top of the forward Boiler Room they distinctly heard the noise of tapping above all the others. Eventually they located the source of the noise as on the starboard side and in the Low Power Room under the flooded deck on which they were standing.

Action to pump out this water was taken immediately, and as soon as the level was sufficiently reduced, chain blocks were hooked on to the armoured hatch cover. The repair party then hauled on the tackle and slowly hoisted the hatch open. Then up through the opening climbed two electrical artificers. They had been trapped for so many hours in this small space that the air was nearly exhausted. Their survival seemed like a miracle. They owed their lives partly to their own automatic and intelligent action in keeping the power going, even though all other means of communication had been severed, and partly to the enquiring eyes of the Torpedo Officer, had not the routine structural examination by the Shipwright Officer found them first.

That night, as hot food was not yet available, permission was again granted for rum to be issued. The emergency store was under lock and key in the Victualling Office forward. A party of volunteers, intensely willing, was found and they made their way through the darkness and chaos on the messdecks to this department. The rum jars were collected and taken aft to the Paymaster's cabin, from the doorway of which the issue was made. One jar however never arrived. The loss of the rum had to be investigated, but nothing in the way of conclusive evidence could be found. All the prime suspects appeared to have been affected by a sort of inspired ignorance and the culprit was never caught.

Some years later the true story came out. On the way

aft one of the party placed his jar behind one of the rafts lashed to the hangar bulkhead and then discreetly disappeared. Several days later when all the hullabaloo had died down, the culprit returned, posted look-outs and had a ball. The instigator, a certain Chief Petty Officer, had to be carried back to his mess in a state of complete intoxication.

It was not until the first of April that the last of the merchant ships finally arrived, making 14 in all to complete the voyage. Over a quarter of P.Q.13 had therefore been lost by enemy action. It was also disappointing to learn on our arrival about the merchant ship *Tobruk,* which after getting parted from the convoy had relied on her speed to get there on her own. This she had done, but she was now lying on the bottom having been hit by a bomb during a raid, shortly after dropping anchor.

Only *Silja* of the three Norwegian whalers was heard of again, eventually being towed in by the *Harrier*. It was feared that top weight formed by the build-up of ice had caused both *Sumba* and *Sulla* to capsize.

To summarise the situation: *Trinidad* had been severely damaged and temporarily put out of action by her own torpedo, and the *Eclipse* badly mauled by enemy gunfire. To set against this the Germans had lost the large modern destroyer *Z.26,* and another had been badly damaged. In addition a U-boat, the *U.585* had been sunk.

The concentration of enemy destroyers, submarines and bombers on P.Q.13 clearly demonstrated the importance the German High Command attached to cutting this supply route to Russia. P.Q.13 was the first convoy to be subjected to the full force of this determination, and at a time when daylight hours were lengthening. Both the merchant ships and their escorts had the right to be proud of the parts they had played in bringing the greater part of such a convoy through. The next chapter will go to show what this convoy meant to the crew of one of the merchantmen, who did not get to Russia. The role of the escorts was very demanding. The *Fury* for instance, with Lieutenant Commander Campbell in command, was closed up at action stations continuously for three days and nights. During that time, she had been rounding up stragglers, beating off dive bomber attacks, chasing German destroyers and finally scattering the U-boat concentration outside the Kola inlet.

Captain Saunders had achieved his objective; but at the cost of nearly losing his ship through an almost unbelievable stroke of fate. Many thousands of torpedoes must have been fired in the course of the Second World War. *Trinidad's* was the only one to come back and explode in the ship that had fired it.

8

The S.S. Induna and the U-boat

Leaving the *Trinidad* preparing herself for dry dock, we take the reader back to the merchant ship *Induna*. This ship, early on the 26th March, found herself alone and some 65 miles ahead of the main group of the convoy. Later that morning with the great storm slowly subsiding, she fell in with the *Empire Starlight* and the Panamanian, *Ballot*. A small escort vessel also joined the little group. This was the *Silja* of 200 tons, which was being sent as a present from the British Government to the Russians.

About 3 p.m. that day, the look-outs reported a lone plane approaching from the East. The poor visibility produced by the incessant snow squalls made it impossible to establish its identity. It came in low and on a steady course directly towards them. Among the officers and crews of the four ships speculation grew with every second that passed. Could it be a Russian plane sent out to look for a part of the incoming convoy? A reasonable assumption, now that they were only some 400 miles from the Kola inlet, or was it an enemy plane?

Junker 88's normally attacked from overhead in a headlong dive, and Blohm and Voss reconnaissance planes usually persisted in observing from a discreet distance, circling around on the horizon. The aircraft droned steadily on, holding its course on the starboard beam.

On the *Induna,* gunner Jackson, with his crew of six at the Bofors gun, tightened his fingers round the trigger, his eyes lining up the target through the gate and cartwheel sights. It would be foolish to take any chances. As the aircraft closed, it turned away to port to complete a tight circle round the four ships, with the guns tracking it round. Jackson loved this gun. It was the best anti-aircraft weapon on the ship. Given half a chance, the slim 16 inch long, three pound shells could certainly destroy an aircraft.

Jackson was not satisfied. He somehow had a growing suspicion that all was not well with this intruder. His No. 2

gunner, also lining up on the target, kept repeating, "On target...on...on...on..." The plane turned again to make another approach at only 200 feet and about 300 yards distance. As it did the visibility suddenly cleared. From somewhere on his right a look-out yelled, "It's a bloody Jerry, he's coming in on..." The rest of the sentence was lost as the Bofors exploded into action. The one clip of four shells was sufficient. The first round hit the engine cowling and ricocheted with a piercing whine, the second struck the starboard engine with a bright orange flash, followed by tongues of flame and clouds of thick black smoke, with the other two shells ripping open the side of the fuselage. Lurching sideways and rapidly losing height, the plane swerved violently away into a snow squall, to disappear from view. There was no confirmation that they had brought it down, but the odds were against it making its way back to Norway.

The instant elation which everyone felt after this success was gradually dispelled, and replaced by the sobering thought that the German pilot would without doubt have reported their position to his headquarters.

Early that evening, with the weather conditions temporarily improved, three specks were seen on the distant horizon, and this sent the gun crews hurrying to their action stations. As the ships grew nearer, it was seen that they were part of the scattered convoy, and as they took up station they identified themselves as the *Effingham, Dunboy* and *Manna*. The little convoy was now made up of six merchant vessels and the escort *Silja*.

All through the next day, the 27th March, they were receiving positions for rendezvous by wireless and accordingly steered to make these rallying points. But at 9.30 a.m. on the day after, a few Junker 88's flew in. There were heavy seas running and intermittent snow squalls and the Germans made a rather timid attack on the group. Perhaps the gunnery reputation of the convoy had already become known to the attackers. In any event, after receiving some 40 rounds from the Bofors and a stream of bullets from the Hotchkiss guns, all with a great deal of accuracy, the planes flew off without inflicting any damage.

Another call to action at noon the same day brought dismay to the crews, when a cruiser and a destroyer were sighted approaching from the westward. If these were German ships, then this would be the end. One can imagine their relief when it was discovered that the ships were part of their own covering force, *Trinidad* and *Fury*. These two ships, after picking them up by radar, had left the main section of the convoy 60 miles further west and had come to check that all was well. After staying with this group for about an hour, the two warships turned back to cover the following convoy.

At 1.30 p.m. the German planes returned. The sound of aircraft could be heard clearly overhead, but, owing to the low cloud, nothing could be seen. Suddenly a twin engined plane dived out of the clouds and attacked the *Ballot*. The plane, a Messerschmidt 110, roared down in a determined attack with his engines full on. At a height of about 300 feet, he dropped a stick of bombs very close before pulling out of his dive. All the ships opened fire with every available gun and the plane flew off to the east. Minutes later another aircraft attacked the *Manna*, dropping four bombs which straddled the ship, and then made off.

The *Manna* was able to continue with the group, but the *Ballot* slowly dropped behind. The near misses had buckled some of her plates. Rivets had burst and seams opened, flooding some compartments. The escort *Silja* circled her for a time, but as the convoy steamed on, the two vessels became lost to view in a snow squall. By this time the master of the *Ballot* had decided to play it safe two ways. He ordered 16 of his crew to take to the boats, while he organised the remainder into a damage control party to contain the flooding. The *Silja,* still in close company, was soon able to pick up the crew in the lifeboat, and, with the assurance of the *Ballot's* master that he could cope with the emergency, turned eastward to rejoin *Induna* and her consorts. The *Ballot,* it was learned later, reached Murmansk under her own power.

During the evening of the 28th, the Captain of the *Empire Starlight* suggested to the Captain of the *Induna*, who was the Vice-Commodore, that they should steer further north, and this was agreed. At midnight the Second Officer Mr. Rowlands, taking over the duty watch on the bridge of the *Induna,* reported to the Captain that they had come to the ice, and was given in reply, "Carry on course". The thin carpet of pancake ice made no appreciable difference to the speed of the vessels,

Imperial War Museum

Convoy passing through pack ice. Note the seal in the foreground

which ploughed on steadily through the night. At least the danger from U-boats should surely be reduced in these waters.

During the Mate's watch between 4 and 8 a.m., events developed rapidly. The *Silja* came alongside and asked if they would give her a tow, as she had now run short of fuel. She also requested that the *Induna* should take on board the men they had picked up from the *Ballot's* lifeboat. After several fruitless attempts, the tow was at last secured and by the first light of the morning of the 29th, the *Induna* set off once again steering due south, her position being 72°N, 38°E.

As the hours passed it became clear that they had ventured too deeply inside the ice barrier. The thin pancake ice floes now gave way to really thick ice, which eventually became a solid field; and this brought them to a halt. The other ships asked them if they could get out and, after receiving an assurance that they would be alright, turned round and left them. With some skilful manoeuvering, the crew slowly worked the *Induna* around in the ice field, broke free, then went to get the *Silja* clear. After going alongside, they took off the 16 men of the *Ballot* — bringing their own complement up to 66 — and started towing her again. At 3 p.m. the two ships were clear of the ice field, with 250 miles to go to the Russian coast.

There was now a rising sea due to a freshening wind. Although *Silja* lengthened the tow line, the weather got worse and the little vessel sheered about a great deal. The great strain generated by these conditions parted the chain cable at 8 p.m. After hauling in what was left of the cable, the *Induna* turned to search for the *Silja*. Lights were flashed, whistles blown and the crew shouted, but they could find no trace of her. They continued the search until 4 a.m. on the 30th, but the visibility in the frequent dense snow squalls was so poor it was impossible to find her. There was nothing more that they could do, but proceed on their way and report the position by wireless. This they did and some days later, the minesweeper *Harrier* found the *Silja* and towed her safely back to Murmansk.

Optimism rose among the *Induna's* crew with every hour that passed. Although free of the ice field, they were still close enough to it to assume that U-boats would hardly operate so far north. They also had the comforting possibility that ships of the following convoy might meet up with them. At their present speed another 24 hours would see them anchored snugly in Vaenga Bay. The wind had risen to near gale force NNW, producing a rough sea; another factor which could lessen the likelihood of enemy action.

No-one saw the tell-tale silvery wake of the periscope that was moving in on their starboard beam. The U-boat commander must have viewed the scene with some degree of incredulity. A careful survey round the horizon would have shown him that there was no other ship in sight — it was all too simple. No-one even noticed the track of the torpedo on its way to strike the starboard side well aft in No. 5 hold. This ignited the cargo of gasoline and the resultant explosion threw everyone off their feet. Flames shot up to a tremendous height and in seconds all the after part of the ship was a blazing inferno. The two Bofors gunners, who had just come on duty on the poop deck, ran, jumping through the flames until they were clear. The remainder of the gun crews however were still in their accommodation on the deck below, and must have perished instantly.

Minutes after the alarm had sounded, the starboard lifeboat was lowered. By the time Mr. Rowlands had destroyed the confidential papers and reached the boat, it was full. Indeed it was overfull, as the extra 16 men from the *Ballot* also had to be saved. Each of *Induna's* lifeboats had a lifesaving capacity of 25 men, but now would have to embark 33. The Chief Officer shouted from deck and ordered the boat to row away from the ship and lie off at about 200 yards. The port lifeboat, although it had been lowered safely into the water, was proving very hard to keep alongside. The men who had already climbed into the boat were being choked by smoke from the fire, which was being fanned by the strong wind and blown straight towards them. The Chief Officer therefore ordered them to go round the stern to the starboard side and take off the remainder.

As they were pulling away, three hundred yards on the starboard beam and only 100 yards from the starboard lifeboat, the black dripping hull of the U-boat slowly surfaced. It was a large craft and appeared to be about 250 feet long. She had a jumping wire and was armed with a small 20 mm gun just forward of the conning tower. The number 140 was clearly visible. The men in the boats watched her, speculating with apprehension, as stories had reached them of U-boat crews machine gunning survivors in boats. In contrast to this, there were also reports of them distributing provisions and blankets, before bidding survivors "Good luck" when they left them. What sort of crew had fate given them on this occasion?

The submarine edged in towards the burning ship, firing a second torpedo into the starboard side which exploded in No. 4 hold with a tremendous blast, lifting the ship and discharging a mass of debris into the air. As the men in the boats waited, the stern of their ship settled rapidly and the bows began to rise high out of the water. They looked on in horror at the efforts of the remaining officers and crew to launch the small jolly boat; but they could not free the falls which had frozen up. In the confusion of the roar of escaping steam, internal explosions and the sound of inrushing water, the bows rose higher until they were almost vertical. Then stern first she plunged straight down, taking the men left on deck with her. From the time the first torpedo had struck to her final disappearance had been just 30 minutes. For some minutes after that the U-boat stood off, then moving forwards she submerged and was lost from view.

In the crowded starboard lifeboat the men looked across the heaving sea for their comrades in the other boat. All they could see was the endless waste of tumbling seas. There was little time to hang about, because it was as much as the Second Officer could do to prevent the boat from falling into the troughs broadside on to the waves, even when the crew was rowing as hard as it could. It was as well that the force 6 wind was astern and blowing them in the direction of their destination, Russia.

A sober assessment of their situation gave Mr. Rowlands little ground for optimism. They were about 175 miles from land, fully exposed to sub-zero temperatures in an open boat and subject to gales and snow storms without warning. Loaded with 32 instead of the capacity 25 men, they were grossly overcrowded. Not only would the men be unable to take exercise to keep warm, but attempts to row would also be hampered. The boat herself was leaking badly and this, added to seas breaking in over the side, required constant baling with buckets to check the rising water level. In his own mind, he had to admit it would be a race against time. How long could their bodies hold out against exposure to the wet and the cold before they were rescued? To the men, he presented a cheerful and optimistic picture of their chances; they had food and water and the following wind if assisted by sailing and rowing, would help them on towards the land.

The men seated on the thwarts were the most fortunate, because the exercise of rowing kept the blood circulating. It was sheer hell for the rest. The injured lay on the bottom boards in freezing water. One of these was the donkeyman, who had been severely burned and was now in great pain, every jolt of the pitching boat adding to his torture. Others sat propped against the sides or perched precariously in the bows; while the remainder managed to bunch themselves together in the stern sheets.

Taking charge, Mr. Rowlands decided to hoist sail. Considerable time elapsed before they were able to step the mast and set the jib-sail; the trouble being that he was the only one who knew how to handle a boat, as most of the men in this boat were from the boiler room.

> *This little boat adrift in Arctic seas,*
> *These frozen men in which the germ of life scarce breathes,*
> *What courage when each hope has almost gone,*
> *To force the whispered cry "we must hold on".*

In this manner, the little band of survivors set out on their long haul to Russia on the morning of the 30th March. Although the boat was running before the wind, the men rowed in spells to keep as warm as possible. But when night fell it grew much colder, and hands became too numb to grasp the oars any longer. In the boat's lockers were 7 bottles of whisky and these were passed round to combat the cold, with a warning to only drink sparingly. Unfortunately, some of the men drank a great deal of the spirit and becoming drowsy fell asleep, some of them into too deep a sleep.

As the grey streaks of dawn appeared, those who had survived the night roused themselves to face the next day. It was soon discovered that not only had the donkeyman slipped mercifully out of this life, but 6 of the older seamen who had drunk deeply the night before, were lying stiff and frozen and would not wake again. With the chill awareness that any one of them could suffer the same fate in the hours ahead, the remaining men lifted the bodies of their shipmates over the side and saw them float away. No-one dared to express to another the growing anxiety and gnawing fear that was rising in their own heart.

All that day they sailed on, occasionally assisting their progress with ever-weakening attempts to hold and pull the oars. The insiduous effects of frost bite were undermining their endeavours. None of the men were wearing sea-boots, which meant that their feet and ankles were in water all the time. The foresail was unlashed and rigged as a shield against the wind and water on the weather side of the boat. The boat was fully stored with milk tablets, biscuits, chocolate and the like. Although the men were not very hungry, the chocolate was appreciated and a few biscuits were eaten. However everyone craved water to drink. The water in their containers was as might be expected, frozen into solid blocks. The only way to get at it was to break open the containers and as there was no way of melting the blocks, then to suck lumps cracked off them. Even the pemmican among the stored food was frozen into unmanageable masses. This like the water had to be hacked into pieces with knives, not an easy task with frozen hands.

That evening, with the sharp lesson of the previous night very much in their minds, the men took only a small sip of the whisky, before settling down for the night. In the ensuing misery and discomfort of the swirling snow and biting wind, everyone felt the cold penetrating deeper and deeper. Early the following morning, Wednesday the 1st April, Mr. Rowlands' roll call revealed that two more had died during the night. It was only with the greatest difficulty that the bodies could be lifted out and placed in the water.

As the day developed the crew looked out over the turbulent water with growing despair, wondering how much longer their bodies could withstand such exposure. From the original 32, numbers were down to 23. While the Second Officer steered, the rest huddled together as best they could. In this way they could get some shelter from the wind and some mutual warmth from each other. A few men's legs had become so numb that they were unable to move without assistance. During the afternoon one of the greasers slumped over his oar and then rolled over into the bottom of the boat. An hour later a steward, one of four men in the bows, slid forward into a coma from which there would be no recovery. These two had to be left where they had fallen, as by now no-one had the strength to lift their bodies over the side.

As dawn of the fourth day broke, any hopes of seeing a coast line were dashed by the sight of the unbroken monotony of a heaving grey sea. Four more men had lost their fight for survival during the night, and only 17 men remained alive. As the hours of daylight passed and early evening approached with the prospect of another cold remorseless night, the last few shreds of hope were turning into utter despair. Only the hardiest men with the staunchest spirits could have lasted this long; were even they to be taken?

Just before 6 o'clock with dark upon them, one of the crew in the stern saw something and pointing south, mumbled something about a ship. All eyes scanned the dim horizon in the failing light and found something there. Mr. Rowlands using his binoculars with shaking hands studied the object with all the presence of mind he could muster. The men watched him with quickening pulses. It was impossible to identify at first, it was at least five miles away and it certainly was not a ship. Suddenly it dawned on Mr. Rowlands what it was. Hardly trusting himself to speak, he turned to the others and said, "Lads, it's a lighthouse — we've made it."

In fact it was Cape Sviatoi lighthouse on the eastern coast of the inlet. Even in their extreme weakness they managed to reach out and clasp one another's hands. Too exhausted to cheer, the men wept openly. The adrenalin of hope ran through their veins like fire — they were going to be alright. Almost within minutes they heard the sounds of planes approaching low over the water. Soon three Russian fighters were clearly visible and they flew around the boat several times. After acknowledging the flag which the crew held up, the fighters flew back to the coast to bring help. At 8 o'clock, just two hours later, a Russian minesweeper came alongside to take them aboard.

Their numbed and swollen legs gave them no power to stand. Their earlier exhilaration had drained the little strength remaining in them and left them frozen effigies of living beings. In this helpless state they could not get themselves out of the boat. The Russians had to come aboard to fasten the ropes used to hoist them on to the ship. One by one, they were carried into a warm messroom, stripped and then wrapped in thick woollen coats and given hot coffee and vodka to drink.

The minesweeper after setting course for Murmansk had made a small detour towards the east during the night. While the rescued survivors of the *Induna* slept, the Russians came across another boat with survivors, this turned out to be the port lifeboat. There were only nine men remaining in this boat; the two Bofors gunners, five Americans, a fireman and a steward's boy, all of whom were picked up alive. Shortly after reaching Murmansk however, on the 3rd April, one of the Americans and the boy died in hospital.

From the *Induna's* total number of 66 men, therefore, only 24 survived. After some weeks of treatment 6 of these were able to walk and were later sent home to England. Many of the remainder, who were kept in hospital at Murmansk, unhappily had such severe frostbite that they had to have feet or legs amputated. Although the last ship of the P.Q.13 convoy arrived in the Kola inlet on the 1st of April, it was not until two days later that the arrival of the last survivors allowed this tragic chapter to be brought to a close.

9

Murmansk and the Vital Railway

In the Kola inlet is the Russian naval base of Polyarny, in the Bay of Vaenga, near the river mouth; while Murmansk itself is situated up the river. This port, 2,000 miles from Scapa Flow and 200 miles east of North Cape, is the only one on the North Coast of Russia capable of being used throughout the year. Archangel, 300 miles further east, freezes up in the winter, and ships can only enter with the help of an icebreaker, a slow and tedious operation.

Only one railway line ran south from Murmansk. This single track line, formerly insignificant, had now assumed the utmost strategic importance for both sides; as it provided the means of transporting the cargoes from the Russian Convoys to beleaguered Leningrad and the Russian central front.

The railway snakes across the Kola peninsular for 150 miles, skirting the multitude of lakes which dominate the landscape there. This brings it to the port of Kandalaksha at the western extremity of the White Sea. This was the most vulnerable stretch of the line, running as it does between the natural boundary of the sea and the Finnish frontier only 50 miles to the west. From there the line continues for a further 250 miles, running south-east along the southern coast of the White Sea, to the town of Belomorsk. There it turns south for 500 miles, holding a course parallel to the Finnish border, at a distance of about 150 miles. The much threatened stretch that ran between the great lakes of Onega and Ladoga was known as the Karelian front. The line then used to end at rail junctions in the vicinity of Leningrad, and from these, trains could be re-routed to their final destinations along any of the tracks radiating from there.

The Finns had succeeded in cutting this railway line in the vicinity of Lake Onega in August, 1941. The Russians had then to construct a loop running east from Belomorsk to join up with the line between Archangel and Moscow. After superhuman efforts on the part of the engineering and rail construction gangs, and despite the appalling conditions experienced on the southern coast of the White Sea in winter, the new line was opened in a very short time and supply trains were once more getting south with their invaluable freights.

One of the most important sources of raw material for Germany was the rich nickel ore mining area of Petsamo, on the Barents Sea coast of Northern Finland. Ore carrying ships operated a shuttle service around North Cape, then south down the Norwegian coast to German ports. This traffic was harassed by our submarines. The nickel ore, together with Swedish iron ore, was vital to the German war effort and they had to maintain the supply whatever the cost.

The German occupation of Denmark and Norway secured both the Baltic and their northern flank; and thereby greatly improved the safety of the ore traffic. The Führer however was still obsessed with the fear of an Allied invasion of Norway, leading to a link up with Russia in the North. If this happened, Germany would inevitably lose the Petsamo mines. He therefore formed the Army of Lapland, later to be known as the German 20th Mountain Army. These 180,000 troops were under the command of General Dietl, whose task was to hold the Petsamo area and operate alongside his ally, Finland, who had been at war with Russia since 1939.

The introduction of convoys to north Russia had stiffened the Russian resistance, so that the German advances on the Eastern front had slowed down. While Hitler was doing everything possible to stop the convoys, he also had to cut the rail link, and the stretch in the Kandalaksha area was the place to do it.

As early as December, 1940, operational plans to do just this had been conceived. Once again, Hitler over-ruled his General Staff and ordered Dietl to take Murmansk, secure the whole Kola peninsular and cut the line as well. If successful, this operation, which was known as "Silver Fox", would not only terminate the flow of allied aid, but could be the start of an outflanking movement round the Russian armies further south. On paper it looked a straightforward task, as the German and Finnish forces together outnumbered the Russian by two to one. But wars are not fought on paper; the three widely separated German thrusts eastward, which then developed, were a failure. The Russian Army units, though outnumbered, had the advantages of strong artillery, short lines of communication and fought from well prepared defensive positions.

The weakness of the whole German strategy in Finland lay in poor communication and supply. There were very few roads and only one single track railway serving the central area. Elsewhere pack mules supplied the troops. The direct sea route to Finland through the Baltic was unusable in the winter when the Gulf of Bothnia froze up, while at all times there was a lack of German merchant ships. In the spring of 1942, the 14th Soviet Army under the command of Lieutenant General Frolov, held the Northern sector that included the approaches to Murmansk and the Kola peninsular. In the previous June, Frolov had only two rifle divisions and a hastily formed third, made up of conscripted civilians and sailors. These were thrown into the defence of the port; and though inexperienced, were enough to stop the Germans a few miles from the town. By the following April he was strong enough to attack Petsamo with the Russian Navy supporting him. However he was repulsed, and from then on the front remained static, apart from a number of localised actions.

Had the Germans succeeded in cutting the railway line at Kandalaksha and infiltrating the Kola peninsular, the convoys would have had to be diverted to Archangel. This would probably have put an end to them, as it would have meant a greater reliance on summer passages as well as a further 300 miles of punishment.

The rail link remained a frequent target. The supply trains and the line itself was attacked by the Luftwaffe, destroying locomotives, derailing trains and smashing the permanent way. The Russian repair gangs, working round the clock, made good the damage as soon as it was inflicted and kept the supplies rolling south.

In retaliation, fighter aircraft flew regular patrols from the Russian airfield at Vaenga, close to Murmansk, whenever the weather and water-logged state of the runway permitted. Vaenga was an unusual airfield, consisting of a long narrow cutting through the pine forest. The hangars were rough sheds under the trees each side of the dirt runway. Many R.A.F. personnel spent long months at this bleak station teaching the Russians to fly and maintain the Hurricanes, which they operated from here.

It was at this time that *Trinidad*, critically damaged, limped into Murmansk. This base, while offering adequate shelter, only had limited repair facilities. Even these, the Russians had refused to share with the Allies until 1942; even though the ships and the men in them were being sacrificed to bring them war material. The Russians were at last compelled to allow us the use of their dry dock, making *Trinidad* one of the first Allied ships to dock there.

The front line was just over the wooded hills nearby, barely 20 miles away. The German air bases at Kirkenes and Petsamo were only a few minutes flying time away. At night, gun flashes from the front could be clearly seen. Hour after hour the enemy bombers came flying over to keep a constant attack of the docks and the installations surrounding them. To counter this the Russian fighters took off from Vaenga, giving rise to series of dog fights in the skies above us. Any hope of relaxation after our recent exertions were quickly dispelled by all this activity in the air. The ship's company had to stay at action stations to act as fire and repair parties to deal with any hits that might be scored on us. The intensity of these air attacks were a measure of the available air power the enemy had built up to prevent the convoys getting through and their cargoes getting south.

Arrangements to de-ammunition the ship could not be made until the 5th April. This also meant that the Walrus aircraft and, much to our relief, 6,000 gallons of aviation spirit had to be off-loaded and placed under Russian protective care until our departure. There were no cranes to lift off the aircraft, which had to be manhandled off the ship and round the dockyard to the river. Here the water level was several feet below the bank, so the Russians built a wooden slipway, using little wood-axes to cut and shape the timbers. Eventually the plane was trundled down this primitive incline into the water and towed away to the Russian seaplane base at Grasnia.

Captain Saunders offered the Russians the services of the Walrus and two of his most experienced officers. In this way a daily sweep of the approaches to the Kola inlet could be made. The Russians accepted gratefully, but regretfully told us that they had lost the lighter, in which the Avgas was stored. Every day for six weeks the Pilot would go along and ask

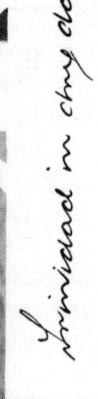

Trinidad in dry dock at Rosta

if he could fill up with petrol and carry out an anti-submarine sweep; but until we were due to leave, the answer always was, "Ah, Mr. Thompson, we are very sorry, but we have lost your petrol barge. Perhaps tomorrow we find him – eh – perhaps?" And yet throughout our enforced stay, merchant shipping was being sunk in the very waters the Walrus could have been searching.

To be near their charge, Lieutenant Thompson and Sub Lieutenant House, the pilot and the observer, lived in a block of flats at Grasnia, while the ship was in drydock. Their recollections include a pleasant raisin tea and the services of a very attractive female interpreter. She was called Myra Brunovitch and came from Leningrad. Though she had never been out of Russia she spoke excellent English, but once she was most embarrassed when she was asked if they had public houses in Russia. Mistakenly, she had thought certain establishments, long outlawed in Soviet Russia, were meant.

The Germans were attacking Grasnia regularly by air. During one of the air-raids a Ju 88 dropped a stick of heavy bombs down the line of the three block of flats, in which they were living. One of these bombs pitched just outside the end of their building. All the windows and half the wall came crashing in, but the pilot was firmly established under a four-poster bed and the observer was just as safe, flat against the wall behind a wardrobe.

At last, on the 7th April, *Trinidad* was slowly moved into the graving dock at Rosta. As this dock had been built to accommodate merchant vessels rather than warships, there was some doubt if the cruiser would clear the sill at the entrance; but with only inches to spare, she did.

The authorities were singularly unhelpful and merely allowed us the use of the dock on the understanding that we carried out the docking arrangements ourselves. The incessant bombing of the dockyard installations had destroyed practically all forms of power. If it was ever true that necessity was the mother of invention, it was true then. It was a Robinson Crusoe circumstance calling for Heath Robinson expedients, but they worked. The ship had to be pulled by ropes into the dock by her own crew. Once there, massive tree trunks had to be cut to size by the ship's crew to shore the ship in place between the dock walls. Calculations of weights, stresses and

116

Torpedo damage Starboard Side.

The port side torpedo damage

The hole is 50 ft × 20 ft.

Left: The port side torpedo damage. The hole is 50 ft. x 20 ft.
Right: Torpedo damage starboard side

strains normally worked out by specialised dockyard draughtsmen, now had to be done by our team of shipwrights under the direction of the Warrant Shipwright. With no internal power available in the ship, any lifts normally performed by cranes had to be done by manpower.

As the water was gradually pumped out of the dock, the full extent of the damage could be seen. The huge gaping hole, where the torpedo had struck the port side, was about 50 feet long and 20 feet high, and there was considerable distortion running forward and aft from there. Three decks, upper, platform and hold, were laid bare. Some of the bulkheads had completely disintegrated, while others had been driven through adjacent ones. Sections of 3" and 2" armour plate had been ripped out like sheets of paper, slicing through decks. A part of one of these sections had been doubled backwards and outwards, until it extended like a large fin out through the hole. In the starboard side opposite, another hole 10 feet by 8 feet, its edges blackened by fire, gaped wide open. It was through this hole a marine had been blown by the force of the explosion and had survived. Well aft, near the water line, there were the two shell holes, which had been plugged with hammocks to keep out the sea.

A cursory survey of the main torpedo damage, by the Damage Control Officer, showed that some of the messdecks no longer existed. Many compartments were flooded in such a way as to seal off the compartments beneath them. Generally the damage to ladders, the tangle of wreckage and heaps of equipment and fittings made it most difficult to get about in the zone of the disaster.

A party had to be organised to recover the bodies of the 32 men in the lower compartments. Despite the gruesome nature of the task, a call for volunteers brought a ready response and a party, mostly of marines, was formed. Suitably dressed, they were assembled under the supervision of the Captain of the Royal Marines, to make the descent. Among the first to enter the damaged area were Marine Douglas and Able Seaman Norsworthy. They found the quarters around the Royal Marine Barracks a mass of twisted and tangled girders. Sheets of steel had been ripped from the bulkheads, and the deck gashed open in long jagged slits. As his eyes travelled over the scene, Douglas saw a hand, fingers uppermost, in a gap in the deck.

As he approached, he was horrified to find it was only a hand, which had been sheared off at the wrist, with the body lying some distance away. As the party searched, so more and more bodies were found, distorted girders had to be cut away with oxy-acetylene equipment by Blacksmith Frank Firth, to release bodies that had been trapped in the wreckage.

The unpredictable effects of the explosion were demonstrated by the discovery Stoker Petty Officer Shepherd made on entering the Sectional Damage Control Headquarters. It was as if nothing had happened. The scene was a complete contrast, chairs and tables were undisturbed, showing little evidence of the enormous eruption which had taken place in the Barracks nearby. Yet everyone of the Damage Control Party who had been at their action stations in the compartment, had disappeared. It seemed logical to assume that these men had rushed out through the door in the bulkhead into the darkness of the mess, where the deck had completely disappeared leaving a hole 20 feet across. They must have fallen straight through this into the sea and been carried away.

The most distressing and harrowing experience for the rescue party was the recovery of those who had been in the Transmitting Station. Here, one officer, 15 Royal Marine Bandsmen and two writer ratings had been killed, drowned in oil fuel when the bulkhead gave way. The oil and water had by now been pumped out, allowing the men of the party to lower themselves, one by one, into the vault like space, which reeked of death and fuel oil. Guided only by the eerie light of the temporary equipment, the grim tableau that now met their eyes was as tragic as it was sickening; even to those in the party who had experienced the inevitable results of battle.

Two bodies were half way up the ladder, their arms locked round the rungs. However, most were lying pathetically collected together at the foot of the ladder, up which they had tried to make their escape. Among them was that likeable little Welshman, Arthur Evans from the accounting section. He was a deeply religious man, who only a few days earlier had confided to Petty Officer Ken Hitchcock that he felt he would not return from this trip.

The party then found in one corner of the space Nat Gould, the officer who had been in charge. The aftermath of death had dealt strangely, yet very gently with him. As the oil level had slowly fallen when it had been pumped out; so it had lowered him very carefully into his accustomed chair. He was lying back with his feet resting across a box, as though he had fallen asleep.

Eventually the task of recovery was complete, and it now fell to the duty of Royal Marine Sergeant Feltham, with the help of the Master-at-Arms, to collect all the personal effects from the recovered bodies. Each article was carefully set aside, cleaned and put together in bundles for forwarding to the next-of-kin when the ship got back to England.

The following day, the British minesweeper *Niger* went to sea, carrying on her quarterdeck 32 crude coffins covered with Union Flags. There at the mouth of the Kola inlet, the customary naval burial service was read as *Trinidad's* dead were committed to the sea. In the minds of those who watched crept the thought that "there but for the grace of God....." On *Niger's* return the Chaplain held a short memorial service on the dockside. In the hazy light of a bitterly cold evening, the group of men from *Trinidad* listened to and participated in the service with the sincerity that stems from the comradeship that existed between them and those who had died.

A tradition in the Navy, which has existed for at least 200 years, is the sale before the mast of a dead shipmate's uniform and non-personal effects to provide funds for dependants such as widows. The Master-at-Arms, whose duty it is to conduct such sales, had taken off his own woolly hat, prior to conducting the auction. It was not until it was too late, that he discovered he had sold his own hat along with the other effects to the highest bidder, much to the amusement of the men and the new owner.

The Ordnance Staff now had the messy job of stripping out the fire control equipment from the Transmitting Station. Every bit of it was covered with oil fuel and the conditions of work were most arduous and unpleasant. Working in relays, the various assemblies were removed, cleaned, packed and labelled. The only packing material available was oakum, which is the name for the teased out rope yarns that were once used for caulking the seams of wooden ships. Prisoners in H.M. Naval Prisons or "Glasshouses" had to pick one pound of oakum a day as a punishment, and the work was very hard on the fingers. Such was the urgency of the need for oakum however, that the Ordnance Staff were picking something like three pounds a day, with the result that their finger tips were soon raw and bleeding. As Ordnance Artificer Warren said afterwards, "It put us right off jail for ever."

One personal dilemma of the Paymaster Commander was his discovery that after the action the keys of the main safe were missing. These were normally attached to his trousers by a chain. He retraced his steps and looked in all the most likely places where the chain might have hooked up, but without result. Eventually he broadcast to the ship's company, to ask if anyone had picked up a bunch of keys. If so then they should be sure to let him know. They were the keys to the safe and without them, he regretted there could be no payment next pay-day. The keys were useless by themselves, as only he knew the combination of the safe. About four days later, when consideration was being given to breaking open the safe, the Master-at-Arms came along with the missing keys. He had heard the broadcast, but it had meant nothing at the time. During the previous night, he had woken in the small hours, remembering that after the action he had picked up a bunch of keys outside the Cypher Office and placed them on top of a locker. He immediately got up and rushed down to find them just where he had put them days before. Payment took place as usual.

It was clear to all at Rosta that the silhouette of the cruiser in the dock and against the surrounding snow would be conspicuous to the enemy. Any air survey on the dockyard would attract the attention of the German pilots to *Trinidad* and concentrated bombing was bound to follow. In an effort to deceive enemy reconnaissance the Russians co-operated in the construction of a colossal scheme of camouflage. On the 8th April, every officer and rating who could be spared from *Trinidad* was set to work, fetching hundreds of planks from nearby timber yards. Once at the ship, carpenters rigged the planks into vast platforms over each of the triple gun turrets. Enormous nets and sails were then hoisted between the masts and funnels to distort the more obvious outlines of a warship. Sheets of canvas were suspended over the gap between the ship and the dock wall, and these were painted white to blend in with snow covered areas all around. From the air the plan view of the ship and the dock were still evident against the white surroundings. So three wide tracks of black ashes were led from the roads nearby, up to, across and beyond the cruiser to simulate roadways crossing the area.

Most of the labour force employed at the timber yard were women, strong square shouldered, muscular amazons. Any one of them could pick up a couple of planks with apparent ease, while we men could just struggle along with only one each. The ashes were collected from the gas works, up in the hills. Here our working parties filled up large wooden boxes with cinders, and they then gleefully pushed them downhill over ice tracks to the dockside for spreading. By the evening everyone was congratulating each other on the splendid job that had been done. But there were groans of dismay the following morning, when it was discovered that a heavy snow fall overnight had covered all the cinder tracks, and that we would have to repeat all the work of the previous day. Whatever else might be said about the primitive efforts of the Russians in other directions at Murmansk; there was no doubt that they were masters of the art of camouflage. The whole scheme was dealt with in the most comprehensive manner and the effectiveness of the camouflage was conclusively proved by aerial photographs taken of *Trinidad* later on.

The first and most important task was to patch the great hole in the ship's side. The outcome of Captain Saunder's approach to Russian Dockyard Officers at first seemed to be satisfactory, as they claimed they had sufficient suitable steel plate to complete the job. However any early optimism was soon dispelled by the Russian's refusal either to show him any plates, or to give him any date on which a start could be made. In the face of such uncertainty he had no alternative but to signal home for plates to be sent by the next convoy. Actually the Russians had the plates somewhere in the yard, but had mislaid them under the snow and would have to wait until this melted to re-establish their whereabouts.

In due course, as in any other dockyard, a start was made by the dockyard work force to repair the damage. A few women welders were sent along, who proved to be skilled at their job; but very much under the influence of their overseers as regards their attitude to the work. They were made to carry on working until 10 o'clock at night, when they would lie down alongside their job and go to sleep. In the morning they were awakened by their overseers coming along and giving them a kick to start them working again. They rarely seemed to leave, except to get food. Even then, they were organised into groups and marched away. Among these women was one named Katerina, a forewoman welder, who was really the political leader of the gang. For an hour each day, she would stimulate them to greater efforts by giving them a political pep-talk. The bulk of the repair work was however done by our own staff, who achieved remarkable results under almost impossible conditions.

While the Russians could and did do a very good practical job in helping us patch the ship's side; they did not seem able to plan ahead. Having welded one plate in position, they would then go away to have a think about how to deal with the next one. So the work did not proceed smoothly. At the rate we were going, it looked as if we should be in Murmansk until the war was over. The Admiralty therefore sent out Constructor Commander Skinner, who arrived in the *Liverpool* with the next convoy, to do the planning.

Some of the merchant ships anchored in the river, waiting to be unloaded or convoyed home, became desperately short of food. A seaman in one of these ships wrote the following about an experience he had during a foraging expedition.

"One day we put down our jolly boat and rowed down river to an American ship, to try and cadge some fresh stores. While on board the Germans started dive bombing the harbour. Several of us stood on the deck watching the action. With bombs falling all around someone happened to ask one of the Yanks what cargo they were carrying. "Ammunition and black powder," was the reply. Immediately there was an almighty rush over the side into our jolly boat, despite the water around us being peppered by shrapnel and gunfire from the attacking planes. We rowed like the very devil to the so called safety of our ship, which was loaded with petrol."

"What a choice: to be blown up or burnt up? It is truly remarkable how often, in crises like these, there is an absurd and senseless reasoning, which at the time seems so important, but overall, matters little. I suppose we felt we would rather be with our own shipmates, if anything like that was going to happen."

At this time of year the Arctic winter was occasionally interrupted by a spring-like day, which pierced the black grey roof of the sky with thin watery shafts of sunlight, as if to herald better weather. Even so the bitterly cold winds from the Siberian lowlands persisted, whistling with penetrating blasts over the Kola basin in defiance of the warmth and sunshine to come.

Even though the weather might be showing signs of improving, the cold atmosphere in the unheated ship was only one facet of the severe and cheerless conditions, under which we had to live. Food was desperately short. A survey of the damage to the food stores proved to be a great blow to the Supply Department. As a result of action damage, sea water and oil fuel had filled these sections and this included the cold room. As the access door had been damaged the entire stock of meat had been contaminated and the cooling machinery wrecked. Water had also flooded into the forward storerooms, destroying all the reserves of food stowed on the decks. Luckily the cool room had stood up to the blast, and its contents were less badly damaged. The recoverable food from this room was therefore disembarked, and to keep it fresh as long as possible; it was buried in the snow with an armed guard constantly in attendance.

It was explained to the ship's company that a severe scale of rationing would have to be imposed throughout our stay. This was generally accepted with good grace. However there was one instance when a famished rating was driven to protest to the Paymaster Commander; saying that though it might be alright for an old man like him, a youngster like the rating needed more. The age of the two men being 39 and 26 respectively.

Dinners sometimes consisted of a 90% watered down soup, described as "Yak Ugh." Each plate contained two or three small strips of Yak hide, which was like well seasoned leather. The Yak, a sort of Russian ox, was our only source of fresh meat. Often on a Sunday morning one of these animals was brought down to the dockside and shot, skinned and cut up to provide us with meat. Unfortunately it was so tough the only way to deal with it was to boil it into some sort of stew. The result was likened by the crew to a mixture of salt water and oil fuel.

Lieutenant Commander Herepath, the First Lieutenant, introduced a new feature into the usual naval routine. This took the form of a one day conference of all the Leading Hands of the Broadside Messes, together with the Petty Officers of the Messdecks and himself. The leading hands were able to raise any constructive suggestions that might improve the domestic arrangements in the ship. It was understood that there could be no criticisms levelled at senior officers or orders issued by them. Early fears that this might happen and provide a field day for messdeck lawyers were unfounded. On the contrary, the get-together proved to be most successful and this attempt to improve conditions was greatly appreciated.

However low our own food stocks were, the Russian citizens were far worse off. The gaping hole in the side of our ship was an open invitation to the starving, to try and reach the meagre supplies which were still intact inboard. These poor souls were really desperate and made nearly suicidal attempts to climb into the dock to reach the stores through the opening. Royal Marine sentries had to be stationed at strategic positions on the upper deck, to discourage these intruders with warning shots.

On one such occasion, Sub Lieutenant House observed a small party of Russian workmen. They were furtively creeping out of the hole, loaded with stores they had filched. On his instructions, the sentries fired a few shots over their heads, whereupon the men dropped the parcels and fled. The following day one of the Commissars came down to the ship, shepherding a party of small children. After claiming that these were the desperate band of thieves who had invaded the ship, he added, "It was most regrettable that the British should have opened fire on small helpless children"; which no doubt inferred recriminations and diplomatic intervention.

A few waste bins were usually placed near the ship on the dockside. When the buckets of sloppy waste, known in the Navy as gash, were emptied into these bins; a crowd of Russians would assemble. They would dip their hands and arms deep into this gash and gather up as much as they could carry. To them it was a feast. The carcasses which we had thrown out of our cold room had been condemned by our doctor as highly poisonous and far too dangerous to eat. The starving Russians thought differently. Under the cover of darkness they risked the shots of our sentries and retrieved every scrap.

One old Russian was not so alert or so nimble as the others. Before he could escape, he was shot by one of the Russian guards and died on the dockside beside the carcasses. On another occasion a dockyard workman picked up a tin of jam, which had fallen clear of the ship's stores while they were being sorted on the quay. Thinking he had not been seen, he hid the tin under his coat and made for the dockyard gates. A watchful Russian guard challenged him. Foolishly the workman started to run and without further ado was shot.

During the voyage to Russia, those in the crew who had strong communistic sympathies had openly expressed their views on the "Great way of life" in the country we were going to. This often led to some fairly vociferous arguments in the messdecks. But after a period of careful observation of the "Great way of life," the same men appeared to undergo a complete change of heart. The "hot gospellers" of communism, thoroughly discouraged by all they had seen, lapsed into silence.

Among the privations we had to bear was the local water supply, and typhoid fever was rife in the area. In addition to the precautions taken to control the drinking water, every man received an anti-typhoid injection. The inevitable aftermath of this innoculation was twenty four hours of violent shivering, which was particularly severe without the comfort of any sort of warmth.

To start with, makeshift latrines had to be rigged for the ship's company out on the river ice. Each one of these contained an essential implement, a larch pole. This was used to break the ice, in the absence of a chain to pull. This was a time when the weather was very bad, and the men usually went out in small parties, because of a pack of wolves that hung around. Later the shipwrights constructed some wooden shacks on stilts. These were on the foreshore overhanging the river. The comfort of these luxury heads was spoilt by the seat holes being cut so far back, that one's legs stuck out straight in front. In any case, it was so bitterly cold that visits were only made when it was absolutely essential. There was a situation created by a "full house" on one occasion. All the holes were seen to be supplied with bottoms, getting bluer and bluer. Outside a little queue had formed to wait their turn.

Nearby there was an old Russian peasant, armed with a shot gun, who was shooting seagulls for food and for the feathers, which were stuffed into jacket linings for warmth. One of the gunner's mates standing in the queue, decided he couldn't wait any longer. After a little persuasion, he borrowed the Russian's gun and fired a round under the seats. The effect was most impressive, for all the bottoms rose as one and within seconds the place was empty.

Furthermore, with all the snow around, it was generally accepted that an exposed bottom might be subjected to a barrage of well-aimed snow-balls at any time. When a missile found its target, the air would be rent with volumes of curses and howls of rage. The recurrent offence of "Skulkin in the 'eads" that the old lags get charged with, never seemed to arise while we were at Rosta.

Some of the sentries became affected by the intensity of the light reflected from the snow after a few hours on duty. Royal Marine Tom Culley was on duty as a sentry once when he was approached by the Officer of the Watch and asked if there was anything to report. Culley replied, "It would be alright if I could see you Sir." He had become quite snow blind during the first hour of his watch.

The only form of outdoor entertainment was sleigh riding. The sleighs were crude, but they still gave plenty of enjoyment. This was alright as long as the sleighs were kept to the proper worn paths as ordered, but there were times when "Jack ashore" decided that he'd like to explore. On numerous occasions these excursions caused the Russian guards, posted on the ridges of the hills, to open fire. It was only by the most extraordinary feats of acrobatics, tumbling down hills and weaving from side to side, that these sailors ever survived to reach the safety of the ship. We learned that sometime before our arrival, two British merchant seamen had been shot in similar circumstances.

We found the ordinary folk anxious to be friendly; but the commissars and guards appeared to be suspicious and resentful. Murmansk was only a few miles away and most of the crew made at least one trek into town to buy a few momentos. The town had suffered severely from the effects of incendiary and heavy bombing attacks and had not had time to recover from them. A few square and unattractive buildings had escaped the bombing and stood out grim and harsh among the ruins. Only here and there could one find the odd shop or store.

The usual method of transport into Murmansk was to hitch a lift in one of the many passing lorries. This had the disadvantage that German planes quite often flew low over the road, machine gunning anything that looked like a target. So everyone had to be ready to scramble out and take refuge under the vehicle. On one trip into town, Able Seaman Jim Peters and two of his friends boarded a covered van which had stopped for them. They settled themselves down on what appeared to be a soft bench. In the dim light of the interior, they could vaguely make out three fur coated Russians seated on the other side of the van, with rifles across their knees. From the sign language and pidgin English which followed, it became apparent that they had returned from a bear hunt. When asked about the result of their expedition, the Russians roaring with laughter pointed to the comfortable seat beneath our chaps. The speed with which they leapt to their feet, was only matched by their look of utter astonishment as they peered down at two huge black bears, on which they had been so comfortably reclining.

In town we were often met by Russian youngsters aged from about five upwards. Using a combination of words and gestures they asked for chocolates and cigarettes. What we had we gave, but from some of the unlucky ones, we received abuse, even, "..... you Jack, I'm alright". Our minesweeper crews obviously had been here well before us.

At one of the stores I had a rather alarming experience while buying two or three items. The purchasing system in the store was for the selected item to be put aside on the counter. A bill was made out and handed to the purchaser, who took it to the pay desk. Here a receipt was given in return for cash. This had then to be taken back to the counter and exchanged for the purchased item. I had already gone through this involved procedure twice. On purchasing the third article, I must have been given the wrong receipt at the pay desk. Because, when I presented the paper to the assistant at the counter, a very ugly scene developed. The assistant called out to two Russian guards at the door; one of whom seized me and the other pressed the point of a bayonet into my midriff. All my letters and private papers were pulled from my pockets and thoroughly examined. Eventually, after the problem had been sorted out, I was allowed to go free. Several hours later, a very relieved ordinary seaman arrived back at the dockside, thankful to see the camouflaged outline of *Trinidad* again.

An experience the Chaplain had was even more alarming. Eager to take every opportunity to learn the language, he went ashore armed with a notebook and pencil. A foreigner in a dockyard in wartime, walking around with a notebook in hand, was of course looked upon with the utmost suspicion. Challenged by the guards, he was asked to produce his identification papers. These included a photograph of himself, taken when he joined the ship at Devonport. Menacing with his rifle, the sentry made the padre raise his hands, but every time the padre tried to lower them to retrieve his special pass from his pocket, the rifle was pushed threateningly in the direction of his stomach. It was some time before the pass with the photo was handed to the sentry. During his service in the Arctic, the Chaplain had grown a magnificent black beard, which would have put any Greek Orthodox priest to shame. The photo on the pass now bore no resemblance to the man in front of the sentry. In a matter of minutes a dispirited and rather nervous Chaplain was led away, and despite all his protests placed in a cell overnight. Even in peace time, Russian prisons are not the best places to be detained, but under these conditions it must have been particularly grim. Eventually, through the intervention of Captain Saunders and the British base authorities, he was released.

The suspicious attitude of the Russians, magnified by the language barrier, fostered many unfortunate incidents; however they made one or two efforts to improve relations. One instance of this, was the arrival of a Red Army choir, who gave us a memorable evening's entertainment in the spacious hangar deck. The choir comprised some thirty singers and the final item, a rendering of the Volga Boatmen, brought the audience to their feet in appreciation. Perhaps the circumstances coloured the occasion, but I have never heard this national song sung so well. The Russian entertainers were taken along to the Wardroom after the show, for drinks and refreshments. Needless to say, they had their political commissar with them. Even he, after a few gins, participated in the general hand shaking, back slapping and embracing; and later there was an exchange of hammer and sickle brooches for those with *Trinidad's* crest. A good time was had by all.

The hangar was also used to put on a ship's company concert. Lieutenant Commander Hodgson was the director, using all available talent, with the First Lieutenant as compere. The entertainment ability while not brilliant, was appreciated by all and went down very well; but as someone said, "What wouldn't, when stuck in a dry dock in a place like Murmansk?" The highlight of the show was the First Lieutenant and two others from the Wardroom, all dressed up like mothers with babies in their arms, singing a comic song.

A film was shown on another occasion and this featured a most glamourous South American lady, who danced in the most provoking way possible. It doesn't require much imagination to conjure up the picture of a large company of sex starved sailors, groaning and grinding their teeth, in a simulated agony of supressed excitement. It nearly lifted the roof off the hangar.

At one time, a drinking contest developed in the Wardroom, between some Russian submarine and British naval officers. This was comfortably won by the Royal Navy, as the outcome of this "na zdarovye" versus "cheers" was a number of the guests being carried back to their ship. No opportunity was missed to make the most of any humorous occurence, which might brighten the sombre surroundings. One evening the Padre had fallen asleep in an easy chair in the Wardroom. The others lost no time in taking advantage of this, by wrapping his arms around two large beer bottles and taking a photograph. The resulting picture gave every evidence that the Padre had been completely sloshed.

An example of the friendly Russian approach occurred towards the end of our stay, when a number of our officers were invited to a Russian version of "Rose Marie". This was a Red Army concert party production and took place in Murmansk, in what had formerly been the Hall of Culture. During the interval the tenor came to the front of the curtains and sang the title song in English. As the song ended, the Russians in the audience rose, turned in the direction of the English guests and much to their embarrassment, clapped them heartily.

In accordance with our earlier requests, arrangements had been made to send steel plates out to us. On the 8th April, P.Q.14 a convoy of 24 ships, sailed from Iceland. Escorted by the cruiser *Edinburgh,* flying the flag of Rear Admiral Bonham-Carter and carrying the plates we so urgently needed. Storms and floating ice so damaged 16 of this convoy that they were compelled to return to Iceland. Of the remainder, *Empire Howard* was torpedoed, killing Captain F. Rees, R.N.R., the Commodore of this convoy. It was not until the 19th April that the *Edinburgh* and her 7 remaining charges arrived at the inlet.

In *Trinidad* we had been looking forward with great expectation to this moment and the food and mail that *Edinburgh* would bring us. She brought neither, only a consignment of boots and attache cases. The bitter disappointment caused by this silly blunder can hardly be imagined. We had to content ourselves with the knowledge that she had at least brought the plates, which had been delivered to Rosta dockyard.

The repairs to the plating could now proceed without any forseeable delay; but the internal stiffening of the hull presented a different problem. All the Russians could and would supply were lengths of timber. These might have been satisfactory while the cruiser lay in dry dock, but would not withstand the forces set up in an Arctic storm. Steel was needed.

The problem looked insurmountable to the Constructor and his staff of shipwrights. Though there were stacks of suitable steel girders in various parts of the yard, they were under the vigilant eyes of Russian sentries. Surveying the possibilities the yard had to offer, all that could be seen from the *Trinidad's* deck were two small cranes, an old railway locomotive which never moved and a system of tracks for it. These went from the dockside, passed under a high wall and out into the periphery of the yard. The gleam of an idea came to one of the leading hands, who must stay un-named. Though they could hardly abduct and demolish the cranes and the loco, railway lines were a very different matter. Cut to the right length, they could be easily transported and would make ideal stiffeners for the plating.

Firstly the rails would have to be dug out of the track and then cut up. As this had to be done without the knowledge of the sentries, a plan was drawn up. The following day, without seeking official approval, nor apparently, with the blessing of the ship's more senior officers, two parties of ratings inconspicuously left the ship.

One party, aptly designed the "Diversionary Squad" was armed with bars of chocolate, and the other, the "Recovery Division" with oxy-acetylene equipment. Within a few minutes her first party had the complete attention of the sentries, to whom chocolate was like manna from heaven. Whereupon the Recovery Division set to work. Inside the hour a considerable stretch of the line under the wall had been cut up. Each portion was concealed under sacking until an opportunity allowed it to be brought furtively on board. In the days that followed this master stroke, the ship's artificers welded the lengths of railway line into position to provide the basis for shoring up. This was then supplemented by timber supports, with cement being poured into cavities and recesses to bind everything together.

This solution also left us with the company of "Casey Jones", the very ancient and decrepit locomotive, already mentioned. This was our only source of power. Fuel was provided by working parties from the ship, fetching supplies of wood from the nearby timber yard; while water came from an old water cart tied alongside. The engine had no shelter from the weather, and was run by an old Russian woman. When the engine had a full head of steam, she would blow the whistle to let us know that power was available.

With the structural repairs making satisfactory progress towards completion, the time had come to protect the steelwork with red lead paint. Gallons of red lead, applied with a multiplicity of criss-cross strokes covered up the repaired section. Some of the ratings seemed to get more red lead on themselves than on the ship. The spectacle of red lead brings to mind a painting incident that took place earlier in the war.

The Captain of the ship involved had a dachsund, which had a habit of creeping up and biting people in the back of the leg. One of the Royal Marines in the working party was duly nipped, and in retaliation he took a hefty swipe at the retreating dog with his paintbrush. The Captain mustered the ship's company and demanded to know who had painted his dog's hindquarters red. As no one would admit to it, he threatened to stop all leave until someone confessed. Later the culprit asked to see the Captain and admitted he was the offender. "What made you do a thing like that?" he was asked. "Well sir," said the marine "the dog attacked me." "How do you mean?" retorted the Captain. "Stern First!"

As the days passed into weeks, the crew's tolerance became sorely tried. Only those who have been cooped up in close quarters with several hundred other men, can fully understand the stresses and strains that build up. Very few letters arrived from home to relieve the tension, and those that did survive enemy action were often soaked in oil fuel. On the momentous occasions when a few letters did arrive, it was a time of extreme emotion. Men could not keep still as names were called. Tears would appear in the eyes of some of those who received mail, and of some who did not.

An envelope with the impress of lipstick, would be passed round quite seriously by a young recipient, for his shipmates to kiss, and each in turn lingered in the process. After this, the letter which would be couched in endearing and personal terms, was read out to an enraptured audience. There was no sniggering of embarrassment amongst these men. Each with his own thoughts was identifying himself with his own loved ones, through the words which were being read. Some would gaze at their own unopened envelope for several seconds, conscious of the physical link it represented and the slender chance it had had of ever arriving at all.

Tempers were often strained on the messdecks. Arguments frequently arose over some trifling issue, and ratings would face one another like ferocious tigers. In one instance the leading hand, merely to entertain the rest, provoked the contestants into more ferocity; then noticing a man kneeling in prayer, as was his custom before getting into his hammock, roared for silence and got it. Then when his prayer was finished, he coerced the men to continue arguing, which they did with renewed vigour. Arguments like this ended as quickly as they began; for often in the middle of the uproar, action stations would sound and they would quickly hand each other their gear.

10

Running the Gauntlet

> "Oh, midnight sun, why not your brilliant
>   beams of light
> Plunge deep, below this freezing Arctic sea,
> That neath the mantle of the covering night,
> We might escape."

Convoys were still being sailed to Russia while the *Trinidad* was lying in dry dock. In fact political pressure from our allies was forcing us to step them up, despite increasing hours of daylight and enemy concentrations, which might have prompted the reverse. Before dealing with the experiences of these convoys, it should prove interesting to take a look at those of one of the locally based smaller British warships, which were doing invaluable work in the approaches to Murmansk.

At about the time of our arrival, the minesweeper *Speedwell* with consorts had been given the task of proceeding eastward from Murmansk towards Archangel, to meet a convoy that icebreakers had taken three weeks to get out. They patrolled in thick ice at the arranged meeting point until eventually they sighted the convoy off Cape Tevski Orloff. At noon that day the Russian destroyer *Kuibishev* exploded a mine in her paravane sweep, doing herself some damage, so *Speedwell* immediately put out her own sweep wires. Later in the day they managed to get clear of the ice and were then able to steam due west. That night they had about the worst job in their experience. It blew a gale and it became particularly difficult to remain in touch with the trudging convoy and keep the ships together. In the morning they found that they were one merchant ship short. Then, as they approached Kildin Island a thick fog came down, so they decided to anchor the convoy in the lee of the island. As far as they knew no U-boats had penetrated in that far; anyway it was out of the question to try and reach the Kola inlet in such thick weather.

In the middle of getting the convoy turned round safely

a patrolling Russian trawler arrived and, getting officious, signalled, "Stop or I fire". *Speedwell's* skipper, fully occupied with his responsibilities, not to say worried and harrassed, snapped at his Russian interpreter, "Tell him, if he does, I'll blow him out of the water". What message was actually sent they never knew, but the trawler gave no more trouble. The work of the *Speedwell* had made the interpreter very pro-British in the few days he had been on board.

On the following day, only a few hours after seeing the convoy safely anchored in the inlet, *Speedwell* received a signal, that a Russian Gromky class destroyer had run out of fuel at sea and was drifting helplessly. The Russian Naval Command were in a dreadful state about it and rightly so, as it would be a miracle if she was not found by a U-boat and torpedoed. When they were told that *Speedwell* would be in the rescue party, they nearly fell round Lieutenant Commander Young's neck, so well spread was his fame as a salvager of disabled ships. In the event, the Russians sent some tugs of their own to accompany *Speedwell* and *Niger* to Bolshoi Oleni (Big Reindeer) Island. They found the destroyer, which was towed to safety with them providing a U-boat screen. A few days later her Captain disappeared; it being rumoured that he had been reduced to Ordinary Seaman.

Three days after docking on the 10th April, Q.P.10, a convoy of 16 empty ships led by Captain D. A. Casey, moved out of the Kola inlet. Among this group were some of the vessels we had escorted to Murmansk. The escort consisted of the cruiser *Liverpool*, the destroyers *Fury*, *Eclipse*, *Punjabi*, *Marne* and *Oribi*, the trawlers *Paynter* and *Blackfly* and the minesweeper *Speedwell*. Although this constituted a considerable naval force, it was also clear that icebergs drifting south would bring the convoy even closer into the range of the enemy airfields. Fog and snow squalls gave protection for part of the voyage, but U-boats and dive bombers succeeded in sinking four of the merchant ships. These included two of our earlier charges, *Harpalion* and *Empire Cowper*. However, the concentrated return fire of the escorts and the merchant ships destroyed 6 German aircraft.

After delivering our steel plates, the *Edinburgh* sailed on the 28th April to escort the returning convoy Q.P.11, which was made up of 13 ships. On the morning of her departure an extraordinary incident occurred. A lorry guarded by Russian sentries halted on the jetty and unloaded a number of pom-pom ammunition boxes. These were then transferred to the security of a sealed compartment on board *Edinburgh*, the working party of seamen carrying the boxes being closely watched by marines. The ship's company, guided by an ancient naval superstition, became apprehensive when they learned the boxes contained gold bullion. Nor were these misgivings allayed, when it was seen that the red paint, which had been slapped across the sides of the boxes, had dripped on to the deck. This bad omen caused the Acting Chief Buffer to say, "God, I don't like the look of that. I think we've had it".

Three days later, 240 miles out from the Kola inlet, *Edinburgh* was torpedoed by the *U.456*. The U-boat had stationed herself ahead of the convoy, and was in a perfect position to fire the two torpedoes which blew the stern off the cruiser. Although she was unmanageable a gallant effort was made to tow the *Edinburgh* back to the inlet. The Russian destroyers escorting her were running short of fuel, and they signalled that they would have to return to base. Further, as it was May Day, their national holiday, they would be unable to provide further assistance for another two or three days. Four British minesweepers then arrived to provide an anti-submarine screen, and fortunately a Russian tug to attempt a tow.

Three German destroyers were directed to the scene, and in the brilliant naval engagement which followed, the *Edinburgh* received a further torpedo, which proved to be her coup-de-grace. A spirited and courageous defence had been put up by the one active turret left on the stricken cruiser. The two British destroyers, *Forester* and *Foresight* were both badly damaged when they came to her assistance. One of the German destroyers, the *Hermann Schoeman* was so badly mauled by one of *Edinburgh's* salvoes, that she had to be subsequently scuttled. Although the two remaining Nazi ships with their superior fire power should have been able to eliminate the escort, they had had enough and broke off the engagement before making for home.

The *Edinburgh* survivors, who included both Admiral Bonham-Carter and her Commanding Officer, Captain W. H. Faulkner, were soon taken on board the escorting minesweepers, which then returned to Vaenga. It fell to the *Foresight* to fire her last torpedo into the cruiser, which broke her in two. She quickly sank, taking down with her 1¼ million pounds in gold bullion. This engagement cost the Navy the lives of 78 men and had wounded 43 more.

Almost exactly four weeks after she had entered the drydock, *Trinidad* moved out into mid-stream on the 2nd May. There were still a few temporary repairs to be completed, but on the 4th we carried out extensive trials in the mouth of the inlet to prove the strength of the considerable body of work that had been finished.

On the morning of the 5th, we watched the arrival of P.Q.15, which had sailed from Iceland on the 26th April. Out of the total of 25 ships in this convoy three had been sunk by enemy torpedo aircraft. This convoy had also been marred by a tragedy, when the escorts sunk the Polish submarine *P.551*, when she was 100 miles out of position.

Rumours of departure dates, cancellations, new departure dates and further delays, were the main topic of conversation between decks in *Trinidad*. Unknown to the main body of the ship's company were intelligence reports of possible movements of German battleships around the Norwegian coast. On the 9th May, Admiral Bonham-Carter hoisted his flag in *Trinidad*, fully intending to sail the same day. However the uncertainty over the enemy's intentions postponed sailing until the situation became clearer. By the 12th May, reconnaissance and intelligence reports indicated that there was no imminent threat from the known disposition of the German warships.

It was about this time that Captain Saunders received a coded message. This told him that, instead of returning to England and some long awaited leave, the ship was going direct to Philadelphia, U.S.A. for repairs and refit. This was because all the dockyards in the United Kingdom had as much work as they could manage. He kept this news to himself, as he realised that it was going to cause considerable disappointment and he wanted time to think of the best way of breaking it to the men. One can imagine his concern, when one of our minesweepers came alongside and started offering our lads addresses of girls in Philadelphia, where they had recently had a short refit. It turned out all this minesweeper's crew knew of our destination and were openly discussing it. Needless to say, there was no question of gently breaking the news to us, but instead there were some hard words said about the security of secret information in a small ship.

We were now ready for sea, or as ready as we ever should be. As far as the victualling situation was concerned, it was time for us to leave. The feeding of the ship's company had become an acute problem. Nearly all the stores were exhausted. In a little while we would be down to a diet of ship's biscuits and the attendant weevils. The Paymaster Commander and his supply staff had done a remarkably fine job to make the supplies last until the day of our departure.

However cheering the thought might be that we were returning to western waters and eventually home, our immediate concern was for the passage we would have to make first. The enemy would be waiting for us in the Barents Sea. This was the danger that had to be faced, the gauntlet that had to be run.

Two close friends of Jim Harper told him that they did not expect to live much longer. They seemed strangely aware of their fate and yet behaved as though all was well to every one else. These two, Arnold Pickup, who had held a responsible position with Spillers, and Harold Breeze, who was a chemist in civilian life, seemed to take obvious pleasure in doing things for anyone about this time.

We weighed anchor just before midnight on the 13th May, in the grey aura of Arctic night as summer approaches. With only the after Boiler Room in operation, we proceeded at our maximum speed of 20 knots as we left the Kola inlet. There was evidence that the patching of the torpedo damage was not completely successful, as a tell-tale slick of oil stretched out for miles behind us. Escorting us were the destroyers *Somali* and *Matchless*. Additional support came from the *Foresight* and *Forester*, which by now had been temporarily repaired. This was a case of the crippled helping each other, because their speed and endurance also had severe limitations.

The Russian Meteorological Office confidentially assured us that thick fog was building up beyond the coast line, and this would give us full cover for a considerable part of the homeward voyage. It was with this comforting thought that we proceeded north. My own action station was to be on the open bridge for the return journey. With this vantage point I was able to view the scene and experience the events as they then developed. As we cleared the mouth of the inlet, we could clearly see the distant wooded hills that the Germans were occupying on the western side of the bay. At intervals we could see signal lights flashing from one point to another. It seemed reasonable to assume that these were signals being made by the German advanced position, reporting our departure: an ominous reminder that the enemy would have ample time to prepare themselves, to prevent us escaping through the dangerous stretch of water between the Norwegian coast and Bear Island.

We had received firm assurance from the Russians of fighter protection for the first 250 miles of the voyage. Three aircraft covered the ship for less than 45 minutes, before this token force disappeared over the horizon towards their base at Vaenga. Without this cover, which would at least have deterred snooper planes, a German reconnaissance plane picked us up at 7.30 the following morning after we had covered only 130 miles. After remaining on the horizon well outside accurate gun range for an hour, the plane must have satisfied itself that there was no convoy following as it began sending back homing signals to its bases at Petsamo and Kirkenes, giving our course and position. It was evident that we could expect a full scale attack within a matter of hours; nor would the thin cloud and infrequent snow showers provide us any worthwhile cover from it.

It was hoped that our northerly course would bring us into the fog patches usually found close to the Arctic ice cap. But they were not there; instead icebergs dotted the horizon. As day wore on the visibility improved and the floating ice barrier made it necessary for us to alter to a course which would bring us nearer to the enemy coast. The occasional snow shower brought us only temporary relief from the eyes of the shadowing aircraft. Emerging from one of these zones of decreased visibility, we found that the snooper had moved in closer to investigage. A few well placed shots from our six-inch and four-inch guns were enough to send it scurrying off to a safer distance.

At 11 o'clock that morning, while still keeping as close to the ice as possible, we sighted the conning tower of a U-boat. This was straight ahead and three or four miles to the north, positioned between us and the ice reef. There was no other alternative but to alter course to almost due west. By noon we had lost the U-boat and were travelling north again, but any chance of escaping in this direction was baulked by the appearance of the white outline of the ice barrier. Once more we turned to the westward.

As we were to learn later, important tactical plans were already being drawn up at Banak; both by Major Blodorn, operating the Junkers 88 squadron K.G.30; and Colonel Ernst Roth, the Flight Commander at Bardufoss, conducting operations of the Air Torpedo group flying HE.111's. In the period we had been in dock, the German air bases had benefited from further reinforcements in the desperate attempt to annihilate every Russian convoy that tried to get through. The strength of the Luftwaffe in the North Cape area had now reached the following figures:-

    103 JU 88 Long range bombers,
    42 HE 111 Torpedo bombers,
    15 HE 115 Torpedo seaplanes,
    30 Stuka dive bombers,
    74 Long range reconnaissance aircraft, (B & V 138 and FW Condors).

The last mentioned, the giant multi-engined Condors were the key to the operation. They were able to fly long range sweeps far out into the Arctic Sea to find the convoys and guide the massed bomber squadrons to attack them.

In *Trinidad* every man stood closed up at his action station with as much composure as each could muster. It is always a chilling sight to see men in anti-flash gear before a battle. The white hoods and long gloves remind one of a team of surgeons waiting to perform a major operation. Meals were taken at action stations and the men were fed at their guns, because there was no other option at that time. The cooks had done a miraculous job in getting some sort of heated food to everyone. They had no rest at all, because when a lull occurred and most of the crew could relax, the cooks had to rush from their action stations to the galleys to contrive a quick meal for the ship's company.

By 7 o'clock that evening two more shadowing aircraft had arrived. The two Junkers and the two Blohm and Voss flying boats were making continuous homing signals to their bases. There was feverish activity on the bridge, as signals were dispatched and received, and reports continuously came in about the shadowing aircrafts' signals. An hour later two submarines were sighted, one to the north against the edge of the ice and another just astern. The vultures were gathering.

Whereas in March we had been able to take refuge from the dive bombers in the snow squalls, there was now no fog, no snow, little cloud and not even any sea mist. What clouds there were would favour the bombers, for they were light misty ones high above the ship, which planes could use to screen their run in for the attack. There would be no darkness to cover us, because so far north there were 24 hours of daylight at this time of year.

At 9 o'clock, the radar operators reported formations of enemy aircraft approaching between the bearings of 180° and 240°, which was between the port beam and off the port bow. The reports to the bridge became more frequent: "A wave of aircraft at 15 miles", "Another at 30 miles", "There are more coming in at 40 miles", "Another wave at 60 miles" and then from the radar room, "The screen is full of aircraft, Sir". It was clear that the three German bases, at Banak, Tromso and Bardufoss had each contributed to an all out effort to attack and destroy us.

The suspense of doing nothing but wait was almost unbearable. I remember the odd sinking feeling that I experienced before *Trinidad* and her four escorting destroyers became the target for these bombers. Men who believe in God commit themselves to his keeping on these occasions; while some of those who have previously scorned religion are often suddenly glad to find they have a God to call upon, however much they have previously denied His existence.

Just before sailing we had taken on board from 80 to 100 passengers. They were mostly coloured seamen from torpedoed merchant ships, but some were survivors from the *Edinburgh,* and there were also a few Polish officers and two Russian officials. So now, way below in the crowded Canteen and Recreation Space, the Indian seamen also began to pray to their Gods — to Allah, to Vishnu and to Shiva, for protection. The babble of voices down there grew louder as the minutes passed and the danger more imminent.

From the bridge, instructions were broadcast to the key members of the crew to disperse themselves around the ship. In the event of damage and casualties, this would ensure that there still would be a nucleus of staff able to take charge and act as replacements.

It was nearly two hours to midnight, and if ever we needed the cover of darkness, we needed it then. But out there the orange red sun hung poised on the rim of the horizon, like a visitor from outer space come to watch the mounting drama. Then its imperceptible descent over the edge of the world was gently checked by the ageless voice of time, calling for the birth of a new day. Obediently the sun began to climb out of the Arctic Sea as one day merged into the next.

The grey desolate waste of the Barents Sea seemed to stretch interminably on and on. Nearly 350 years before, in 1596, the Dutch explorer William Barents sailed through these same seas and died on the return voyage. Little could he have imagined on that lone exploration how these waters would become the scene of many bitter and bloody battles.

Then from out of the southern sky, we heard them. At first a low whisper, merging into a rhythmic hum like a swarm of angry bees. The familiar drone of Junkers planes grew closer and closer. Anxiously our eyes peered into the scattered haze high above us. At the guns, fingers tensed round the triggers as the noise increased.

Just before 10 o'clock they came at us. Formations of 88's screamed down at near vertical angles, to pull out from their dives at incredibly low levels as they released their bombs. We watched with tight throats as the groups of bombs came towards us — nearer and nearer — to miss by only a few feet, on one side or the other. Then came the mighty explosions and towering sheets of water falling across the ship.

The barrage from the combined power of the 8 four-inch guns, the 9 two pounders, the 8 machine guns and the 12 six-inch turret guns produced a deafening roar, to which we became quite insensitive as time passed. The sky became just a procession of aircraft, queuing up to take their turn to attack us. As they expended their loads, they returned to base as more formations replaced them. The action in March had eliminated control through the Transmitting Station, and each turret had to fire independently. The officer of the turret stood with his head stuck out of a small hatch in the turret and directed the fire, which was towards the area of the sound of aircraft engines.

The last hours. Three Junker 88's coming in to attack

But for Captain Saunders astute handling of the ship, swinging her to port or starboard in anticipation of the fall of each stick of bombs, *Trinidad* must surely have been ripped apart. For nearly two hours the attacks were continued without a break. Again and again the planes came snarling down, sometimes singly and sometimes in groups of two or three.

No one dared express the thought uppermost in our minds — just how long could the welded repairs take the battering from these near misses? Each explosion, followed by a shower of shrapnel, sent a massive shudder through the ship, but still the plates held.

Our four escorting destroyers were also receiving their share of attention from the bombers. Sometimes they would be completely enveloped in the columns of water, thrown up 40 to 50 feet in the air by the near misses. However when the water and steam cleared, we could see they were still intact and making their way as steadily as ever. The *Matchless* in particular was receiving more than her share, possibly because she was on the edge of the clearer sky. Just as it seemed inevitable that one particular stick of bombs would hit her, Captain Eaton her Commanding Officer, would judge the right moment to increase speed rapidly, and the bombs would fall astern, exploding harmlessly in the wake.

While our gunners had their hands full fighting off the planes overhead, the torpedo bombers arrived. They appeared as little dots at first, low on the horizon. Their shape and size became clearly defined as they got closer. They were Heinkel 115's and 111's, each carrying two torpedoes. Skimming just above the water, they came in line ahead in a wide circle. Sections of the already exhausted gun crews were now switched on to these new targets, which meant depressing their guns until they were firing downwards at the oncoming aircraft. But still the greater part of the armament was pounding away at the Junkers above.

Whatever plan of action the torpedo bombers had in mind, it was rudely shattered by the intensity of the counter barrage laid down. The whole line of attacking aircraft suddenly swerved away, showing that they had no liking for our shells exploding so dangerously close to them. Minutes later they returned to the attack in line abreast, approaching from the

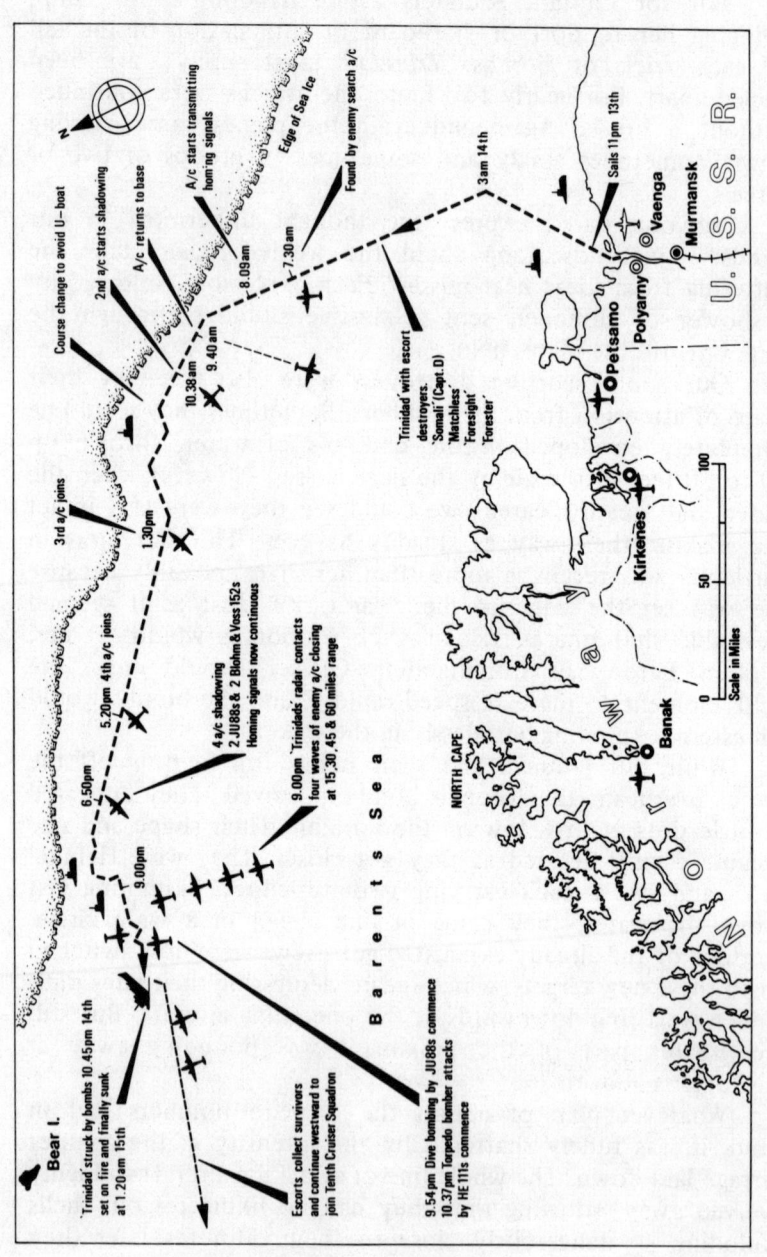

Fig: 9 *The sinking of the Trinidad, 15th May 1942.*

quarter and the beam. Two of the escorts, *Somali* and *Foresight* were ready for them and laid down such a curtain of fire, that the Germans had no resource but to turn away again.

As if the odds against us were not high enough, the lookouts now reported that they could see at least four enemy U-boats deployed to the north and east. But the more immediate danger was still the torpedo bombers, which were gathering for a further attempt to destroy us.

Already twice frustrated, they made this attack in two groups, one on the port and the other on the starboard quarter, releasing their torpedoes almost at surface level. Fortunately the tracks could be seen clearly. *Trinidad* was able to swing clear of their trails, in time to see the deadly tin fish go speeding by on either side.

As though gathering for the kill and determined to be the ones to deliver the death blow, the 8 Heinkels again circled and came in for a further assault on the port beam. On the bridge calmness prevailed despite the pressure of the two pronged attacks. Cruisers however, cannot be made to turn and dodge about as easily as little motor boats, and it was now that disaster caught up with us.

A single Junkers, attacking from the cover of a thin cloud immediately overhead, came roaring down, releasing its load of four bombs at only four hundred feet. Over the speaker system, came the urgent and anguished cry of the Air Defence Officer, "Starboard pom-poms — Starboard pom-poms". But it was already too late.

The cruiser was in the middle of a turn to port, to avoid three torpedoes which were rushing past on the starboard side, but which was also putting her directly into the line of the falling bombs. With the helm hard over and the ship shuddering from end to end, the attempt to avoid them was in vain. We watched with held breath as the bombs grew bigger and bigger. They were coming directly for the bridge, where there was no cover, nowhere to hide or to run; we could only wait for the inevitable holocaust.

The short moment before the bombs struck is unforgettable. The overpowering roar of the plane's engines as it pulled out from the dive and passed over us just above mast head height, or so it seemed. The scream of the wobbling

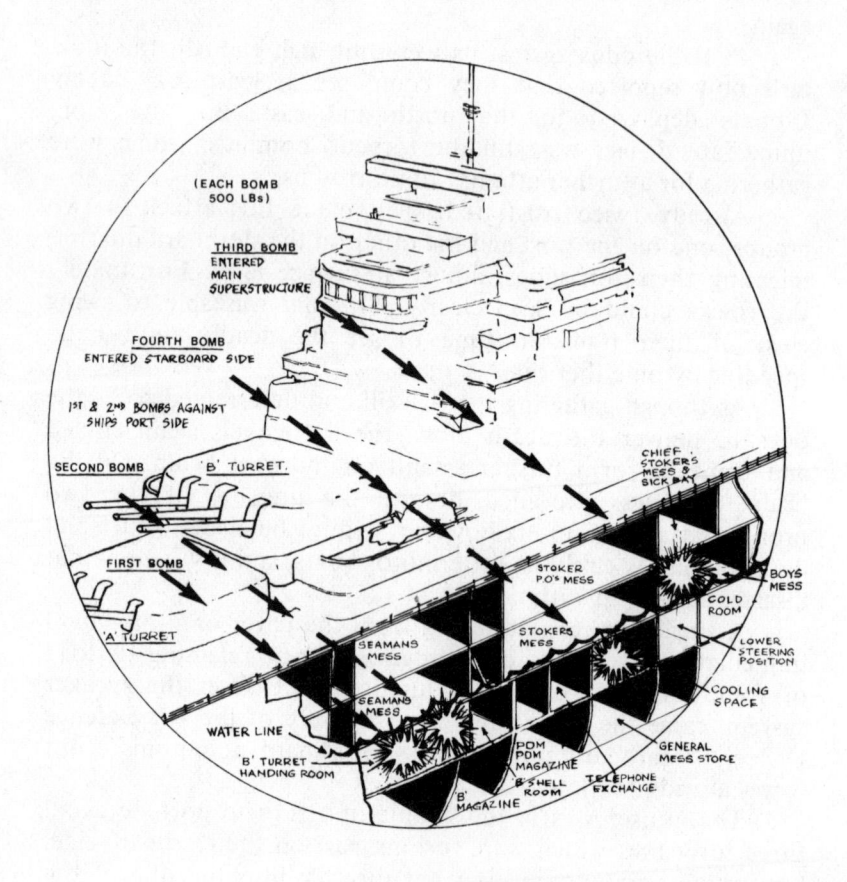

Fig: 10 Where the four bombs exploded.

bombs coming straight for us. The feeling of terror and despair welling up inside. The awareness that our own guns were still roaring defiantly. And, the image of two or three officers with the Captain and the Admiral, facing the bridge parapet with hands at sides — waiting.

Suddenly our little world disintegrated around us; an earthquake which blinded the senses, metal shattering everywhere, the bridge deck leaping, hurling us in all directions. Then there was a sudden quiet, followed by a dawning astonishment that we were still alive.

I found that I was lying on the opposite side of the bridge to where I had been standing earlier. A quick glance round showed me the Gunnery Officer with blood streaming down his face, the Officer of the Watch lying prone and partly stunned, the Captain falling back inboard to the deck, from the bridge screen on to which he had been blown, and the signalmen picking themselves up in various stages of stupor.

Each of the four bombs had been on target. One had fallen outboard, skimming the side of the ship, slightly aft of "B" turret and in line with the bridge. The explosion just under the waterline, had not only blown off the temporary plates, but had sent a wall of water into the compartments under "B" turret. All were instantly flooded, as were the magazine and handing rooms; and all the ratings who were battened down in these areas were drowned. If the bomb had exploded above the waterline, it is certain that flame and not water would have reached the cordite. In which case *Trinidad* and every man in her would have disappeared in one vast ball of fire.

Another bomb landed a few feet in front of the bridge, between us and "B" turret. This entered the ship through the Admiral's sea cabin on the starboard side, passed through the Fleet Air Arm Office and the canteen and exploded in the Stoker's and Petty Officer's messdecks just below this. A great crater, some 40 feet by 20 feet was formed in the foc's'le deck, and all the port side of "B" gun deck was completely blown away. Within minutes the whole of the crater was ablaze, and fire was spreading rapidly to the other messdecks.

The other two bombs had grazed down the port side, outboard, exploding abreast the foc's'le. The combined force of the two blasts produced a sickening lurch. The bomb splinters punctured the forward compartments causing them to flood, while the explosions occurring in the vicinity of the previous torpedo damage, were indeed catastrophic. The already weakened structure and patched-up bulkheads were now torn apart like paper. With tons of water pouring in through the holes in the sides, the ship took on an immediate list to starboard and began to settle by the bow.

The German plane that had caused all this damage, did not get away. The starboard pom-pom gunners had blasted a stream of shells into the aircraft as it dived. Reduced to a streaking fireball, it plunged into the sea away on the port beam.

Trinidad was still able to make reasonable progress, as the ship's after machinery unit had not been affected. Captain Saunders had an agonising decision to make. The torpedo bombers were deploying to make another attack. If he stopped the ship to fight the fires without the wind fanning the flames, the cruiser would be an easy target for the enemy aircraft. If on the other hand the ship was kept going to dodge the torpedoes, the fire might rapidly reach unmanageable proportions. He took the latter course, as there was always the possibility that the fires could be mastered, but there was little chance of the ship surviving further torpedo hits.

11

Trinidad Dies

There were other factors arising from the damage, which contributed to the gravity of the situation. The fire-main forward, which was essential for fire fighting in the area, was found to have been destroyed. All the forward telephone communication system had failed and the revolution telegraph system to the Engineroom had jammed.

The Canteen and Recreation Spaces, filled with the returning merchant seamen, were only a few feet from the place that one of the 500 lb bombs exploded. Few, if any of the men in these sections, survived. Assistant Canteen Manager, Jack Holman, whose action station was close to the Chief and Petty Officer's Mess, had a miraculous escape and takes up the story from here:-

"When the bomb exploded in the next compartment, there was a massive yellow flash. I was hurled forward, hitting the bulkhead and losing consciousness. When I recovered, blood was pouring from a gash on my forehead and a split under the eye. In fact my eyes were so filled with blood, that I thought at first I was blind. The ship was listing over at such an angle that I had to crawl downwards towards the ship's side and from there I stumbled along, blindly feeling my way, climbing over and through the twisted girders and bulkheads which had been torn from the decking. My physical condition was bad enough, but the situation was aggravated by the darkness and the volume of smoke pouring up from somewhere below, enveloping me like a blanket. How I found the ladder leading to the upper deck, I'll never know. Coughing and gasping for breath I managed to make it to the top, feeling the cold fresh air on my face. Suddenly, strong arms were reaching down and pulling me upwards and outwards on to the deck. I must have been the last man out from the area below, the last of only eight, for the Canteen and Recreation Space in which the passengers had been accommodated, had been utterly destroyed."

In this same area a damage control party, which had been assembled at action stations, was completely wiped out.

Just before the bombs fell, eight of the radar operators, who were free of duty now that the Transmitting Station was out of action, were on the Flag Deck watching the bombs fall and frequently taking cover from shrapnel. They seemed well aware it was only a matter of time before hits would be scored. Three of them asked Senior Radar Operator Jack Anderson, if they should stay on up top or find a safer refuge in one of the compartments below. His opinion was that they should stay where they were and they agreed. Remarking that as they had come through the earlier action together in March, if they had to go they might as well go together.

The other four, including Jim Harper, decided it would be safer to go below. It was as they neared the Canteen Flat that the bombs exploded immediately ahead of them, and Harper relates:-

"I lay on the deck, at the foot of the ladder leading to the Captain's sea-going cabin and the bridge. I heard the first bomb go off somewhere nearby and a moment later, another seemed to explode about twenty feet away, throwing a lot of debris over my head. With all this, I was aware of something tearing down through the bridge structure and steel decking, like a machine crashing through plywood. I covered my face with my arms, as a grey shape shot through the deck in front of me. I saw it between my arms. A blinding sheet of flame enveloping me as the iron rivets burst from the deck on which I lay. I was aware of being lifted into the air, with the deck curling round me like paper. Later I came to — how much later I don't know. It seemed very quiet; then high above me, there was a tinkle of a small piece of metal falling. Suddenly I realised the air was hot, in fact the deck and bulkheads which my groping hands touched, were growing hotter every minute. Through the dense billowing smoke pouring out from somewhere just ahead, I noticed the dull glow of fire. With my senses clearing rapidly, I realised I had to get out and get out quickly. I remember stepping through a hole in a bulkhead and eventually finding myself in the hangar space and staggering out on to the catapult deck, to feel the ice cold air hitting me in the face. I was pretty shaken up but still alive and in one piece. I learned later that my three mess-mates who had come below with me, were blown to pieces. Two of them being Arnold Pickup and Harold Breeze, whose earlier premonition had proved sadly and tragically correct."

Replacement damage control and rescue parties, arriving on "B" gun deck, found the area a complete shambles. The gun turret itself had been pushed over to a crazy angle — like a toy that had been smashed by an angry boy — and in addition to the huge crater in the deck, part of the ship's side had also been blown away. From below there were cries for help and men hurriedly lowered ropes. Five were eventually hauled out; one an asdic rating who ran around in circles, vomiting all the time. The limit of the explosion damage reached down as far as the No. 1 Transmitter Room. It was here young ordinary seaman Johnny Cutler found himself as he slowly recovered consciousness; covered in blood from the bodies of two other seamen lying on top of him.

Just forward of "B" gun deck, "A" turret and its crew had fortunately escaped the worst of the blast. The cumulative effect of the shock waves from the four 500 lb bombs, augmented by the near misses along the side, had distorted the ship enough to jam the escape hatches. A vivid description of this has been given by Wardroom Steward Howard Stephens, whose action station was in the magazine of "A" turret, deep down in the ship.

"In these compartments, well below the waterline, any noise in the sea around is greatly amplified by the water. The explosion of the bombs from the near misses along the side of the ship was indeed terrifying. Suddenly, there was one great explosion and I was knocked unconscious. When I recovered, I found I was lying under a pile of cordite cases, for the heavy timbers supporting the racks had snapped. I climbed the ladder and tried to get out, but found the hatch had jammed. I don't think I shall ever forget the dread and dismay that came over me in those awful moments, when I realised that I was trapped in this steel cell and within a ship which was probably sinking. Trying to control the panic which I felt building up inside me, I tore at the dogs and catches of the hatch, but they were immovable.

I recall picking up a small iron bar and banging violently on the metal roof and then shouting at the top of my voice, until my throat could take no more. I could hear the shells rolling about on the deck in the shell room above me and had practically given up hope, when I heard footsteps — someone was up there. The reborn hope gave me new energy to wield my bar and shout. Suddenly there was an answering call, some banging at the hatch and the catches began to turn. Within minutes, the cover was back and I was out and free. My rescuer was able to tell me that he had come back to secure the shells from rolling about. However as we were talking, the increasing list of the ship brought down a whole rack of six-inch shells from one bulkhead, barely missing us. But by now, the hatch out of the shell room had also become jammed. However, there was a possible way of escape through a small opening, in which the shell hoist operated. Shirts off, we squeezed our sweating bodies through the tiny opening and we were free. The deck on the port side, was a blazing inferno, with spouting burning debris erupting from a large crater in the deck, like a firework display."

The starboard Recreation Space below the bridge, had two exits. One of these led to the foc's'le — the other down a hatch to emerge somewhere near the hangar. Leading Telegraphist Ron Bennett had decided to take up a position here, as he felt it would be reasonably safe, sitting on the deck wrapped in a thick duffel coat. He could hear the Air Defence Officer's running commentary describing the air attacks from a nearby speaker. He could also hear the orders being given to the anti-aircraft guns. Suddenly the frantic call came over the speakers for the Starboard pom-poms. The bombs came hurtling down, penetrated the superstructure and exploded somewhere beneath him.

As he regained consciousness, he was aware that his face was stinging and that his left upper jaw felt extremely painful. The room seemed to have gone much darker, with clouds of smoke emerging from the open hatchway. He was unable to co-ordinate mind and muscle. In this semi-conscious state he saw a figure approach, staggering towards the open hatch. Somehow he managed to find the strength to call out, "Keep away!" Who ever it was must have heard, because he turned and staggered through the smoke and gloom towards the foc's'le opening.

Ron Bennett finally managed to get his legs to respond to what his brain was urging him to do; get away as quickly as possible. He realised by this time also, that his feet and ankles were giving him much pain. Slowly he managed to crawl on hands and knees, through the weather door out on to the foc's'le deck. It was only then that he saw where the bomb had struck. A chasm had been made in the deck in front of him and looking down, he could see a fierce fire raging. He could recognise items of messdeck furniture hanging from the ruptured bulkheads and the edges of the decks below. Still on his hands and knees, he found there was sufficient room to skirt the edge of this chasm, and he was able to crawl down the starboard side towards the stern and safety.

Still on his own he continued his slow crawl aft. He became aware of a broken pipe, somewhere up on the bridge structure, which was cascading down a deluge of water right in his path. Curiously enough, despite the pain he was in, his reaction was one of annoyance; and caused him to think, "Hell, I'm going to get wet". However, he went on and was soon spotted by others of the crew, who carried him aft to where first aid was being given.

Although he did not know it at the time, his face and hands had been terribly burned. In addition, his jaw and both his ankles had been fractured and lacerated, and his left eardrum destroyed. A quick examination by the ship's doctor, who himself had a broken arm and head wounds, resulted in a bandage being placed over his face and a shot of morphia in his arm. Later, he was transferred to the *Foresight*, where he was laid out on a mess table and attended to by a Surgeon Lieutenant. Fortunately or unfortunately, he had not been labelled as having been injected with morphia; with the result he got a second dose, which put him out for a very long time.

Reverting to the time of impact of the bombs, Jack Cook, a Coder, felt that the Fleet Air Arm Office would probably be about the safest place in the ship. One of the four bombs came crashing through within a few feet of him. It ploughed on down to the decks below and exploded in one violent upheaval; and relating his experience Cook said:-

"I was suddenly lifted and then seemed to be propelled swiftly into another world, although still held by this one. I seemed to be floating and the image of my wife and little girl floated with me within a feeling of utter tranquility. I felt for my body but it wasn't there — I couldn't see and I couldn't hear, but I could think. After a while, there was a whirling sensation and with a rush, I came back to this world to find myself pinned down by debris, with four others around me, calling for help. Soon willing hands were pulling at the heavy equipment on top of us and carrying us out on to another deck. With others, I was placed by the rail to be taken off in the first rescuing destroyer to come alongside. I was quite blind and paralysed all over; the top of my head had been opened, my right eye damaged and my fingers broken, I felt quite a mess. I think that at this moment, the realisation of my condition brought a sense of revelation, when I was aware that material things were of no avail whatsoever, but there was a spirit which would survive in some form or another."

Just prior to the ship being hit, Able Seaman Fred Manship was sitting calmly inside the Bosun's Locker reading a newspaper. He was a messmate of mine and was always upholding a theory that a bomb or shell would only kill you if it had your name on it. If his philosophy was correct, then the bombs that struck the *Trinidad* must have had the names of Manship and a hundred or more others written all over them.

Inside "B" turret itself the force of the explosion had been so great that bits and pieces of equipment flew in all directions. Captain Griffiths, who was in charge of this turret, ordered one of his marines to shout down to the magazine and handing room crews and tell them to come up at once. There was no reply however and when he and Sergeant Feltham listened at the hatch, all they could hear was water cascading into these compartments. In the shell room directly above these spaces, the water was coming in so rapidly that it was waist high before the last few men could escape.

Able Seaman Wilbourne and some others, who had found themselves trapped in one of the compartments under the bridge, managed to fight their way through to the inside of the hangar. Unfortunately when they arrived, instead of a way of escape, they found the Walrus flying boat well alight. In the confined space and darkness of the hangar, the fumes and heat became overpowering. The Observer made an attempt to turn a hose on to the burning plane; but as most of the fire-main was out of action, all he got was a dribble of water out of the nozzle. In a matter of minutes the situation was quite out of control. The prime consideration now became escape. The only way out was through the heavy hangar doors, but first they had to be opened, by raising them from the bottom using chains. Bomb blast had buckled the doors like everything else and pull as they might, they could only raise them about 12 inches. Fortunately, this was enough and one by one, all of them including the Pilot, managed to slide underneath to comparative safety.

All the while the damage control parties were doing their utmost to put out the fires and restrict the flooding. To counteract the increasing list to starboard, it became necessary to counterflood by admitting even more water into the ship on the port side. This operation had a beneficial if temporary effect as it prevented the ship listing even further and perhaps capsizing, but she was now deeper in the water. Even where the fire parties could get at the seat of the fire, their efforts were hampered by choking black smoke from burning oil fuel. Valiant efforts were made in the area round the Sick Bay, Galley Flats and Damage Control Headquarters, but the intensity of the heat and smoke and the lack of water pressure made the tasks impossible.

Constructor Lieutenant Chatter, with the assistance of a stoker, managed to penetrate as far forward as the Engineroom Artificer's Mess, where they could hear men trapped below shouting for help. They attached a hose to the fire-main, but finding that there was no pressure they sent for protective clothing. This arrived quickly and they put it on before trying once again to penetrate the smoke. The heat was however too great and they had to abandon the attempt.

The fire raging in the hangar had by now heated the deck above to such an extent, that the ready use ammunition was igniting. Pom-pom and machine gun rounds started exploding in all directions, putting up a lethal firework display.

Immediately after the bombs struck, Commander Chisholm-Batten had ordered Stoker Petty Officer Shepherd to make every effort to flood a forward port compartment. Taking two stokers from the after damage control party, Shepherd made his way forward. To reach their destination they had to descend into the main damage area, and if possible skirt round the seats of the fires. To the best of their knowledge these fires were endangering "A" and "B" magazines and might set them off at any time. Actually "B" magazine had flooded and the danger was less than they thought, but their courage was none the less for that. With difficulty they managed to put the flooding into operation, and satisfied that the two stokers could finish the task, Shepherd started his tricky journey back to report to the Engineer Commander.

Leaving Shepherd for the time being, finding his way through smoke filled compartments, wrecked messdecks and smashed bulkheads, we return to the upper deck to find out how the battle was developing.

Although *Trinidad* had been so vitally hit, and obviously this could prove mortal, she was fighting on. There is no quarter given to a sinking warship, and the torpedo bombers were gathering again to attack. Twice more the helm was ordered hard over to present the minimum target of the stern towards the torpedo tracks, which then raced harmlessly by. Five minutes later three pairs of torpedo bombers came in low, just skimming the surface, to release their torpedoes at our port side. Once again, the bright pointers of the tracer shells from the smaller guns gave excellent direction to the four-inch guns. Even though the Heinkels succeeded in dropping their deadly tin fish, their concentrated attack was so broken up by this barrage, that none of the tin fish found their mark.

In the meantime the bridge had been getting more and more discouraging reports from the damage control parties tackling the flooding and the fires. The ship was still listing heavily to starboard and the fires were spreading rapidly through the messdecks, as well as to the hangar and upwards. Further down the situation was as bad. The fires had reached the repairs of the structure damaged previously by our own torpedo, when escorting P.Q.13 to Murmansk. The timber shores and oil fuel leakages were igniting and adding to a conflagration that was already well established.

By 11.30 p.m. the enemy attacks began to ease off, and at last Captain Saunders was able to lessen the fanning of the flames, by reducing speed to 12 knots. By now, even this was too late to do much good. At midnight with the sun just above the horizon, the fires were completely out of control. Down below near the explosion area, those who remained alive, dazed and wounded, were trying to grope their way past flames and through choking smoke to safety. Below them again, were compartments sealed off by the flames as tragically were the men in them. The bridge itself was becoming untenable, as the superstructure was becoming a chimney for the fire below. The flames were roaring up the bridge companion ways and out through the ladder openings.

The state of the ship being so grave, with U-boats in the vicinity and further air attacks inevitable, the Captain decided to abandon ship. Ordering the engines to be stopped a broadcast was made throughout the ship. Commander Collet made the announcement, instructing everyone to muster on the quarter-deck in their respective divisions and warning them not to go back into the ship to collect their personal belongings.

As I left the bridge for the emergency bridge position, I turned to have a last look at the few left up there. Through the billowing smoke, I noticed one of the officers raise his arm to fire a Very's pistol. The green star soared high and hung for a moment like an emerald pendant, before it fell quickly into the sea. The glow of its downward plunge contrasted sharply with the sombre clouds and slate grey seas. This, I supposed was a signal to the escorting destroyers to take off the survivors.

On the emergency bridge, the Admiral and the Captain broadcast for Commander Skinner, the Constructor. He arrived some minutes later, breathless and blackened with smoke. The Admiral asked him, "Skinner, we have ordered abandon ship, were we right?" to which he got the reply, "Sir, it would take the whole Glasgow fire brigade to put out that fire".

Everywhere steps were being taken to clear the ship. Although neither Shepherd or his men had heard the order to abandon, by the time he got back to the Engineer's Office he found the Engineer Commander collecting confidential papers for destruction. On being told, "We've had orders to abandon ship – get your men out quickly!" Shepherd again made his way below, to the compartment where he had left them and brought them safely back to the upper deck. Once there, he along with some others, were ordered to do what they could to reduce the fire round the superstructure. It was a valiant but impossible task, even had it not been abruptly halted when the ammunition on top of the hangar started going off again with renewed intensity. Violent bursts of staccato fire scattered bullets everywhere and drove off the firefighters.

When the order to abandon came through to "B" turret, it was found that the main door out of it had jammed due to the force of the bomb blasts. This meant the gun's crew had to scramble one by one out of the small top hatch, before clambering along the gun barrels, to drop on to what was left of "B" gun deck. By the time they got aft, they found the men who had been rescued from below, lying or sitting around on the quarterdeck near "Y" turret. These men were utterly numbed with shock and had lost the will to move elsewhere. As they sat there, they were being regularly banged against the sides of the turret by the blast of our own guns firing a few feet above their heads.

Deep down in the telephone exchange, below the Stoker's Messdeck, Coder Nicholls, recovering consciousness from the explosions, found himself alone and in darkness. The deck above him had been blown away and the escape ladder with it. On hands and knees he discovered that his two companions had been killed by the blast. No one seemed to hear his shouts. With a stoic resignation to his predicament, he sat down and lit a cigarette. It was this act that saved his life; for at that very moment, a stoker was running through a compartment two decks above. This man happened to look down as he was passing and saw the flare of the match. Soon ropes were lowered and Coder Nicholls was pulled to safety.

When I arrived on the quarterdeck, it was to find most of the survivors assembled. They were waiting calmly in orderly divisions for the destroyers to arrive. How they collected all they had with them, I never found out; but most of them seemed well parcelled up with personal belongings and others had odd bits of food, acquired from the galley. The ship was increasing her list and sinking deeper into the icy water all the time. This made it very difficult to move about, yet morale could not have been higher. Men were even joking about the

"Trinidad" on fire and sinking at 0120 on 15th May 1942

success of their "shopping" expeditions.

One strange and incongruous sight was one of the ratings furiously pedalling away on a wheel-less bicycle. He was presumably from the signals department as he was accompanied by another man with a signalling lamp. This was an emergency method of generating power so that we could communicate with the escorts, which were manoeuvering into position to take us off.

The *Matchless* flying a "G" pendant, was the first to arrive. She nosed carefully in aft of amidships with great skill and due regard for the flames roaring around the bridge and the ready use magazines. All the stretcher cases were loaded on to her decks, followed by many wounded men, who were able to get aboard with assistance from willing hands. This transfer was completed successfully and with courage, as ammunition was still exploding in the fire. The other three destroyers circled round continuously providing a screen to keep the U-boats at bay; very much like chickens fussing around a mother hen. Here and there in the sky, there were still white wisps of smoke like cotton wool hanging in the sky, and the occasional column of water suddenly appearing before falling lazily back into the sea. It was hard to realise that these actually were the results of anti-aircraft shell bursts and exploding bombs.

Radio Mechanic John Evans arrived on the quarterdeck without a coat. Almost at once he was approached by an officer, who asked him if he could spare any clothing to help cover one of the wounded waiting to be transferred. Freezing though he was, he took off his overalls and promptly covered the wounded man, and with three others made up a stretcher party. This team managed to carry two more men to the ship's side, but it was pretty heavy going, as the ship's list was now most pronounced. One of the men they had carried was a coloured seaman, who remained very cheerful even though his heels had been blown off. In the middle of this dramatic episode a man in a sorry condition appeared, he seemed to be blind and not to know what was happening to him. With compassion and great difficulty, they eventually managed to lift, push and pull him over the side on to the decks of the destroyer. It was then that they discovered that he hadn't been wounded at all. The man was extremely short sighted and had lost his glasses. Evans, still only dressed in his shirt and trousers, was climbing over the rails on to the last destroyer to come alongside, when another rating came along *Trinidad's* deck. Although the ship was burning fiercely and sinking slowly under him, he found time to shout across, "Can I interest you in a new line of gent's natty overcoats?" and threw one over to Evans.

A little earlier Shipwright Bert Soper had decided to go down below to collect another coat. On the way, he passed his friend "Blackie" Cass lying down in one of the gangways wrapped in a duffel coat. He said, "What the hell are you doing down here?" to which Cass replied, "I'd decided to get some sleep." Soper hauled him to his feet with, "What! Go to sleep with the bloody ship sinking. Get up top". Passing through the fire area on the way to the upper deck, they were transfixed by the sight of a seaman trapped in a light steel bulkhead, which had been wrapped tightly round him by the force of the explosion. As the flames roared nearer he was screaming his way to death. Every fire-main in the area was out of action and nothing could be done to extricate the wretched man.

It is here I would like to pay a special tribute to a very gallant gentleman, Engineer Lieutenant J. G. Boddy. Some of his stokers were trapped below and could be heard shouting for help. I remember seeing this tall, very young and fair haired officer stepping through a hatchway to the decks below, with the remark, "Can't leave my men below — must try to get them out." That part of ship was by now a raging inferno. There was no ladder and the rope he used to lower himself, must have broken or burnt through. Although a search party was organised, it was driven back by the intense heat. Lieutenant Boddy and the men he had tried to rescue must have perished. He had been married just a week or two before we had left Devonport. Several of his fellow officers and a number of Engineroom ratings had attended the wedding celebration in Plymouth. Now he had sacrificed his life to reach his men; and later in the war he was posthumously awarded the Albert Medal — later to be re-named the George Cross.

Another personality who stood out through this catastrophe was Clifford Avent, our Master-at-Arms. He positioned himself on the top of the after capstan and used a hand megaphone to muster the men into four groups, so each destroyer would get an equal allocation. His steadiness was an example that did much to ensure the success of the transfer.

In quick succession, *Forester* and *Foresight* pulled in alongside the quarterdeck. Moving in orderly groups, we either jumped or scrambled over the guardrails. There were shouts from the *Forester* for someone to dismantle the Oerlikon guns mounted aft on *Trinidad's* quarterdeck. Three Ordnance Artificers lost no time in getting to work on the mountings. In a few minutes, the guns complete with magazines were tied to ropes and hauled over to the destroyer.

George Stripe who was serving in *Foresight* at the time of the transfer described the scene. As they cautiously drew alongside, he could see the whole starboard side of the bridge structure, almost down to the waterline, glowing red hot. It was only when the rescuing destroyers got this close, did their crews realise how fierce the fires really were.

There were sighs of relief from everyone on board *Forester* and *Foresight* when they had taken off their quota of survivors. For by that time, the flames were so close to "A" magazine, that it was in everyone's mind that it only needed a chance spark to blow the lot of us sky high. It was a relief to see that, although there were a few German torpedo and reconnaissance aircraft circling around, the enemy had stopped attacking for the time being.

Petty Officer Sowden was one of the last to arrive on the quarterdeck. The Gunnery Officer spotted that he was carrying a torch, so summoned him to accompany the First Lieutenant in a final search. They went below and searched every compartment it was humanly possible to reach and checked that there were no injured left behind. By the time they reached the upper deck again, the last of the rescuing destroyers, *Somali* was drawing alongside.

It was at this moment that one of the remaining torpedo bombers chose to come in on the port quarter, in a determined effort to finish us off. Away up on the port four-inch gun deck, Commissioned Gunner Dicky Bunt and gunner Charles Norsworthy — known to all as "Nosser" — were manning the guns to the last, to cover the remaining survivors while they climbed aboard the destroyer.

Dicky, running between the port and starboard sides of the gun deck, was the first to spot the oncoming plane. With a shout of, "Nosser, there's one bastard coming in over there," they both jumped on to the port gun mounting and watched the aircraft through binoculars and telescopic sights. The plane, approaching fast, was only about twenty feet above the sea and a mile away when first spotted. All the electrical circuits used to train and elevate the weapon had been destroyed, so the gunners were reduced to the primitive method of laying the mounting by hand. With both barrels loaded they waited.

With the cruiser listing to starboard, they had an additional difficulty when they tried to depress the sights sufficiently to pick up the target. Norsworthy applied his eye to the telescope and directed the gun as best he could. Dicky Bunt in the meantime, peering through the binoculars, was shouting, "Train left — Train left — Stop — Up a bit — Train right" and so on. Changing to look through the open cartwheel sight, Norsworthy lowered the guns a little, to give him a target sighting between the bottom of the plane and the sea; and fired both barrels. It was a masterful effort, for both shells burst about three feet under the plane's port wing, lifting it with such a jerk that it almost capsized. A great cheer went up from the men who were watching. The enemy's torpedo dropped off at a crazy angle, while smoke and flame poured out of the fuselage. Turning sharply away to starboard the Heinkel slowly lost height and disappeared into the sea.

These were the last shells to be fired from *Trinidad*.

The two gunners were the men of the moment. But for their initiative and skill in preventing this attack, the casualties would have been much higher, as it is not likely that the unharrassed torpedo bomber would have missed the stationary cruiser. Dicky Bunt lost his life later in the war, in an action in the Indian Ocean. By a strange co-incidence, Dicky Bunt's father was the gunner and Captain Saunders a Midshipman together in the *Marlborough,* when she was torpedoed at the Battle of Jutland in the First World War.

With the ever increasing list to starboard, the last few survivors were having great difficulty in finding a footing on the sloping decks. Several men were acting as anchor men by attaching themselves to the higher guardrail on the port side. From each of these a dozen or more men hung, clinging together in a human chain, and this prevented men tumbling into the lower scuppers, which were now awash. Lying on deck at the extremity of these chains was Commander Collet. He was directing each man in turn to let go and slide down to the lower rail, before climbing up *Somali's* side.

Able Seamen Charles Ideson and Jim Harper were among the last to make this difficult and awkward climb. They were amused by the spectacle of the Captain's steward jumping for the destroyer, with one hand tightly clutching the Captain's gold braided uniform neatly arranged on its hanger. Here and there one would see suitcases, full of precious personal belongings, flung upwards in an attempt to reach the destroyers decks. Most of these missed their mark and toppled back into the sea between the two ships. As Ideson and Harper's feet touched the deck, they turned round to help those following. Their hands reached down to haul up a rather short chubby man, who was a stranger to them, followed by Commander Collett and, a moment or two later, willing hands were helping up the last man to leave the ship — Captain Saunders.

12

The Last Moments

"It matters not to which side you belong; for in these moments, the sight of a big ship slowly being engulfed by the waves is both tragic and harrowing."

The four destroyers stood off for some minutes to watch the last moments of the cruiser. The canting deck and settling bows revealed more clearly the distressed condition of the stricken ship. Profiled against a background of rolling clouds of black smoke, red tongues of flame from the forward turrets to the catapult deck amidships were ravaging the bridge and superstructure. The fire must have reached the After Boiler Room, for now great clouds of smoke were issuing from the after funnel as well. The huge reeking mass rose from the funeral pyre, high into the sky and, impelled by the gentle westward breeze, rolled away above the grey Arctic sea, to dim the red tinged midnight sun, now climbing out the northern horizon.

To hasten her end Admiral Bonham-Carter on *Somali* gave the unpleasant but necessary order to the *Matchless*, to sink *Trinidad* with torpedoes. Aboard this destroyer, the crew and survivors watched the tubes being trained on the burning ship. When the levers went over, the two steel fish carrying their lethal messages, streaked through the water towards the target.

A breathless hush, which was almost a gasp of despair, enveloped everyone gazing out across the grey stretch of sea between the two ships. In a few seconds the torpedoes were there, embedding themselves into the starboard side of the hull below the bridge. The muffled explosions of the death blows echoed across the water, as the ship, shuddering under their impact, buried her bows in the icy sea. A third torpedo, punching into the same target area, must have almost cut her in two, because three or four minutes later, *Trinidad* slowly moved forward and downward.

From the main and after masts, the large battle ensigns

flaunted their emblems, as if in defiance of the enemy and the leaping flames below them. From a signal halyard on the main mast a short line of flags, already scorched by the heat, fluttered in the breeze, broadcasting her last message to the world, "I am sailing to the Westward".

All around me on the deck of the *Foresight,* a crowd watched in silent thought. Although one could not tell what the other man was thinking, many of them, like myself, were realising that within the sinking hull, a great number of their dead messmates were being committed to the deep. As the water reached the bridge the stern lifted itself clear of the water. There she seemed to hang suspended for a few seconds, as if reluctant to die. Then, with a rush she plunged forward to disappear in an upsurging cloud of smoke and steam. My watch told me it was twenty past one and this was the morning of the 15th May — Ascension Day.

Into the construction of this ship had gone all that was best of modern technical equipment. This, with the men, weapons and machinery had been integrated into a highly sophisticated fighting unit, tested and proved in action. Toil and enthusiasm, endurance and courage, had been the sinews of her existence. Now all that had gone. But the greatest creations are made up of only small parts. My mind returns to those bundles of personal effects which would never reach the next-of-kin of those killed by the torpedo in March.

In minutes, only a widening circle of seething water marked the grave of this new but memorable ship. A fleeting and tragic memorial to a gallant cruiser. In seven months, she had packed more action than many of her sisters which had sailed the seas for as many years. The *Trinidad* would now descend below the surface 1,400 feet to the ocean bed, to lie in the calm darkness of that depth. There she would become shrouded in weeds and entombed in concretions, which would spread over her like a cancerous growth. This lonely war grave would become the haunt for multitudes of sea creatures, which would explore her silent cabins and messdecks for all time.

Away out of gun range, the snooper planes and a few torpedo bombers had stayed to watch the end. It matters not to which side you belong; for in these moments, the sight of a big ship being engulfed by the waves is both tragic and harrowing.

On board the *Somali*, Captain Saunders, helped by the Master-at-Arms, now had the task of assessing the cost of the action in the terms of the dead and wounded. The final result of the official analysis proved to be: one officer and 62 ratings killed in addition to the large number who were seriously wounded. The number killed does not include the Polish prisoners of war and many more coloured merchant seamen, who had been taking passage. Eye witness accounts that have been collected since, make it possible to estimate that there must have been about a hundred passengers sheltering in the vicinity of the Canteen Flat when the bombs exploded. Very few of them came out alive.

At the same time as the casualty list was being drawn up, Harper and Ideson were sitting on the quarterdeck, thankfully drinking the hot tea which the *Somali's* crew had brewed up for them. The short stranger, whom they had hauled aboard from *Trinidad*, then came over and said, "May I be allowed to sit with you chaps?" They immediately made room for him and when he was as comfortable as the conditions would permit, he turned to them with a smile and said, "You lads probably do not know me and I hope you won't throw me overboard when I tell you who I am – you see, I'm rather a Jonah – *Trinidad* is the fifth ship that has gone under me – I'm Admiral Bonham-Carter".. He talked away for some time, until a *Somali* officer came along and asked him if he was the Admiral. Affirming that he was, he left them with, "Sorry, I have to leave you; but this is where I have to put the gold braid on again".

By now the four destroyers, crammed with survivors, were putting as much distance as possible between them and the German airfields. We were becoming increasingly aware of the German reconnaissance planes which never left but shadowed us continuously, tantalisingly just out of range. The speed of both *Foresight* and *Forester* was still limited by the boiler damage inflicted in earlier engagements, so this was the speed of our flotilla.

As I watched the other three destroyers from the deck of *Foresight*, it really came home to me, despite all our tribulations, how thankful we should be that these little ships had been with us and able to rescue us from the sinking *Trinidad*. Away out on the port bow, the *Somali*, carrying most of the officers from *Trinidad*, led the way towards Iceland and safety. No one could have known, that in four months time she was to be torpedoed in these same waters by a U-boat, with the loss of some 40 men. Nor could it have been told that in three months time, Italian aircraft in the Mediterranean would sink the ship on which I was now standing. Only *Matchless* and *Forester* would survive the war, the former to be sold into the Turkish Navy, and the latter to be broken up for scrap as soon as the hostilities were over.

The enemy bombers had not yet done with us. Shortly after we had got under way, another wave of Junkers approached and within minutes were subjecting us to a further bombardment. The misses were far too near for anybody's liking and we were kept busy on the decks of the *Foresight,* playing hide-and-seek on either side of the after funnel, keeping it between us and the shrapnel from the alarmingly near bomb explosions. The fact that we escaped a direct hit was due to the avoiding action taken by Commander Salter. An illustration of his coolness and self control under attack was clearly shown during the short lulls between each stick of bombs, when he calmly picked off seagulls from the bridge, using a home made catapult with dried peas as ammunition.

On deck, one of the few surviving Lascars brought out his prayer mat and placed it so that it was pointing in the direction of Mecca, before prostrating himself to give thanks to Allah for his continued existence.

Below decks, it was hell for the ship's company, but they were marvellous. The gangways were crowded with injured men lying around: mess tables were being used for the more badly wounded, who had to receive medical attention where they lay, yet despite all this the destroyer's crew did their best to prepare some sort of food out of their meagre rations. Teacups were at a premium, and I can recall the great pleasure I derived from sipping hot tea from an old tin with a sharp spiky edge.

The Admiral decided that our small force should seek the protection of the fleet as soon as possible. To this end he instructed a signal to be sent to Scapa, asking the Commander-in-Chief for help from his covering forces. It became the duty of Leading Telegraphist Eric Tubman to send the message. Unfortunately he was unable to contact any shore station, partly due to the great distance involved but mainly because the conditions for wireless working close to the Norwegian coast were particularly difficult. He was instructed instead to make a standard broadcast of the signal to all ships, in the hope that it would be picked up by one of them.

One of the *Foresight's* signalmen kept us informed from time to time on our progress. One piece of information was not encouraging; this was that signals had been received indicating German cruisers, with a destroyer escort, might have set out from Norway, with the clear intention of intercepting and destroying us. Later signals reported unidentified ships approaching from the south and that we should expect sightings in about one hour. Aware that the enemy warships, *Tirpitz*, *Admiral Scheer*, *Hipper* and *Prinz Eugen* could easily sally out from their bases in Norway, anyone who watched the distant horizon did so with anxious eyes. The crews of the destroyers closed up at action stations, loaded their guns and stood ready..

Sure enough, within the hour we could all see eight or nine specks on the horizon. The passing minutes turned the specks into ships as they came closer. One of the watching survivors expressed his concern as to what life would be like in a German prisoner of war camp. The fact that he might not survive to reach the prison camp, did not seem to enter his thoughts; although it certainly occurred to most of the rest of us.

It seemed to us that here was yet another misfortune, and one that could only have one ending. No one dared to express such a morbid thought, because in every sense we were all in the same boat. Instead, the general impression given was one of calm acceptance of the inevitable. But, we were to witness one more example of the tenacity and defiance called for by the traditions of the Royal Navy.

We suddenly felt *Foresight's* deck begin to vibrate more as she increased speed a little and made a tight turn towards the north. *Matchless* and *Forester* came with us, away from the approaching ships. But not *Somali*, because, as she was the only one of the four destroyers left with a full quota of torpedoes, it became her task to make a sweep to the south to meet the oncoming forces. The intention of the plan was evident. If these were German ships, the *Somali* was going to intercept and engage them in a delaying action, which might provide a little time for the other three destroyers to make good their escape to the west.

It would be a sacrificial attempt, which against what must be the superior fire power of so many ships amounted to suicide. The tension and drama mounted as the seconds passed. Here was one destroyer, crammed with survivors, facing up to what looked to be a considerable German fleet, but with only four 4.7" guns with which to do battle. As I watched, I was reminded of Sir Richard Grenville's action off the Azores against the great Spanish galleons, when *"The little Revenge ran on and on".*

Then from the distant ships, we could see little pin pricks of light flashing. Surely these were the first of the gun flashes that we might expect. Gradually as the seconds ticked by, we began to realise that nobody was using us for target practice; and suddenly a great cheer went up from everyone. It could now be seen the flashes were from signalling lamps, which were identifying themselves as being units of our own 10th Cruiser Squadron. It seemed almost unbelievable at first, but as the vessels got nearer there was no mistaking the shapes of our cruisers. Here were *Kent, Norfolk* and *Liverpool,* followed by the *Nigeria* flying the flag of our own Rear Admiral, Burroughs. They were escorted by destroyers and had come to shepherd us back to Iceland.

This welcome squadron had placed itself between the menacing enemy and our vulnerable selves. For this reason its appearance in the sector the Germans would have used was almost alarming. It was a very timely arrival which exhilarated and warmed our hearts.

Within a very short time, our forces had joined to form a wide arrow head, with the four cruisers in the van in two columns; *Kent* and *Norfolk* in the port, and *Nigeria* and *Liverpool* in the starboard. Our own destroyer was on the tip of the port wing of the escorts. Hardly had this formation taken shape when our asdic detected a submerged submarine on the port quarter. Immediately, *Foresight* made a turn to the south and commenced her run in for the attack. When over the area she dropped a pattern of depth charges and made another turn to port. With the echoes becoming louder and faster, the second pattern exploded, once again throwing great mountains of water high into the air. With our cruisers and destroyers moving further and further away, this was no time to hang about chasing U-boats. So without delay the *Foresight* broke off the action; increased speed to the limited maximum and rejoined the squadron; but not before a look-out had reported seeing the bow of a U-boat rise above the surface and slowly sink back.

If earlier the enemy had licked his lips over the tempting morsels presented by *Trinidad* and her four escorts, now he would be drooling at the prospect of the full meal represented by this much larger concentration. From the Luftwaffe's long range air bases at Bardufoss and Banak, formations of aircraft were now taking off for their 300 mile journey to reach us.

Inside an hour the air was filled with the sound of attacking aircraft, diving out of the lowering clouds. The concentration of anti-aircraft fire from the British ships was extremely heavy, yet the German pilots still pressed home their attacks. Roaring down through the blanket of flak in almost vertical dives, dropping their bombs as they levelled off, then climbing out of danger. Walls of water thrown up by near misses would at times completely hide one or another of the cruisers, which were bearing the brunt of the attack. The Germans developed attack after attack; but as the hours passed and the distance from the enemy airfields grew longer, they became less frequent and despite the ferocity of these attacks, the cruisers all survived the blitzing and came through unscathed.

After two days the cruisers left us to take up their assignments, covering the passage of other convoys en route to and from Russia. The last two days of the voyage were uneventful. The ever present reconnaissance plane kept on going round and round on the horizon, only leaving us when we were almost in sight of Iceland. Although it might be reasonable to assume that we would be free from attack during these last few miles, so much tension had been built up during the experiences we had encountered, that I believe no one on deck had slept a wink for the whole voyage. From the time *Trinidad* had left the Kola inlet to our arrival in Iceland, the journey had taken five nightless days. By now the lack of sleep had left us all pretty well exhausted, even though we were buoyed up with happiness to realise that we were still alive.

The destroyers were quickly re-fuelled in the haven of an Icelandic fiord. This gave an opportunity to distribute *Trinidad's* officers evenly among the four destroyers. At the same time, the Captain's Secretary, Paymaster Sub- Lieutenant Hunter and

Petty Officer Writer Ken Hitchcock transferred to *Somali* for a muster of the ship's ledgers, which had been rescued from the *Trinidad*. This muster enabled them to prepare the casualty list signal to the Admiralty. Both men were deeply aware as they carried out their task, it would be only a matter of hours before dependants would be receiving the dreaded telegrams which begin, "The Admiralty regret to inform you..."

We were off again in a few hours, making a detour to skirt the immense mined area between Iceland and the Orkneys. It seemed no time at all before we had arrived at the main anchorage at Scapa, where the numerous wounded were transferred to the hospital ships, *Amarapoora* and *Isle of Jersey*. Here five doctors were hastily transferred from nearby warships to deal with the extra cases. Among the badly wounded was one poor fellow, who had received terrible eye injuries from splintered glass and a Sub-Lieutenant suffering from gangrene, who died soon after.

During our short stay in Iceland, we had noticed a small drifter which anchored quite close to us, but had remained in the fiord till after our departure. Our surprise can be imagined, when having come to our anchorage at Scapa, the same small drifter was seen tying up alongside. Able Seaman Walter Bond called out to the drifter's crew, "You've been mighty quick in reaching Scapa before us." and was casually told that they had come straight through the minefield. Whether this was by design or by accident, no one seemed to know.

Once the wounded had been transferred, the four destroyers weighed and were soon speeding through the Pentland Firth and on down south through the Minches, to edge past the bare flat rocks of the Inner Hebrides and then round the Mull of Kintyre. Soon after, we were experiencing the thrill of sailing up the Clyde on a fine sunny morning. We marvelled at the greenness of the foreground against the purple of the mountains beyond, in comparison with the desolate wastes of the Arctic.

At the best of times the Scottish port of Greenock is no Cannes or Nice, but at this moment it was like entering the gates of paradise; and setting our feet on British soil again was an unforgettable event. One can never forget the kindness of the women of this town, who handed cigarettes and chocolates to every man, as he came down the gangways. A little later, we were sent along to their Memorial Hall, where we were given whatever we wanted in the way of hand knitted pull-overs and cardigans to meet our immediate needs.

Arrangements had been made before our arrival to organise a through train to Plymouth for us. Wearily but jubilantly we settled ourselves in our carriage seats, knowing we were on our way home. As the train pulled away from the station, there stood Captain Saunders waving farewell to the men who had served with him in the *Trinidad*. He could well have been thinking of those who were not on the train and the ship which now lay on the ocean bed. This was the end of an episode, never again would the same body of men experience similar crises together again. Those who had survived would be dispersed, to serve in other ships and fight in other theatres of war in the long months still to come.

Leaning back in the corner of our compartment and realising how tired I was, I decided to have a little sleep. The next thing I remembered was being well and truly shaken and someone saying, "Come along — wake up — Plymouth in ten minutes".

Included in our party was young Johnny Cutler, who, as described earlier, had had a miraculous escape from death in No. 1 Transmitter Room. This experience had left the lad a nervous wreck. Boarding the train at Greenock he had refused to take off his inflatable rubber lifebelt. Only on our arrival at Plymouth could we persuade him to part with it, to find that the belt itself had been slashed open in several places, and would have been utterly useless if he had had to take to the water when abandoning *Trinidad*.

Before long our train steamed into the platform of Drake Barracks station, where we disembarked and assembled into an orderly group, before marching into the barracks centre. The news of our arrival must have got around, because as we marched along between the large stone buildings, crowds of sailors lined the way to welcome our return. Our appearance in our tattered clothing must have given clear indication of the nature of our recent experiences. There were seamen wearing Royal Marine jackets and marines in seamen's jerseys. There were torn oilskins, begrimed duffel coats and oil soaked overalls, marching side by side. The men thus clad might be topped with Russian fur caps, balaclava helmets or hand-knitted skull caps.

174

Survivors on arrival at Greenock

175

Above: Survivors on arrival at Greenock
Right: The Doctor. Surgeon Lt. Cdr. G. H. G. Southwell-Sanders

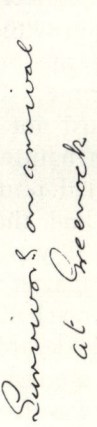

Some men wore seaboots, while others had black leather shoes or even white plimsolls. Illogically, there were still some who had lifebelts around their waists.

We must have looked like something out of a pirates' opera. Indeed, a day or two later, the Plymouth Evening Herald published some details of the return of *Trinidad's* crew, under a headline which read, "The Pirates of Penzance return to Plymouth".

Over and above the cheers and encouraging words from the crowds of sailors all round us, was the feeling that they had great respect and sympathy for all we had gone through. But this was far from the attitude of a very raw Surgeon Lieutenant, who examined one of *Trinidad's* survivors in the Devonport Naval Hospital later. This unfortunate man still suffering from shock, was reliving the torpedoing and the bombing in the form of terrifying nightmares. He was told that his condition could be summed up as, "... all sheer imagination". Soon after, the same young officer was transferred to the Arctic Patrol; and one cannot help but wonder if he ever caught up with the fateful P.Q.17 Convoy. If he did, would his own self-diagnosis have been "all imagination" too?

A similar unfeeling attitude was shown some weeks later, at Kingseat Hospital, where Leading Seaman Bennett had been sent to undergo treatment for his burns and fractures. He had at last been allowed to make his first attempts at walking out into the hospital grounds. Hobbling on crutches, with his head and face still wrapped in bandages, he was accosted by an officious petty officer, who barked, "Hey you, where's your cap?" Fixing him with a steady look, Bennett replied with icy politeness, "At the bottom of the Arctic Ocean, would you like to get it for me?"

But we must not pay too much regard to these displeasing sides of human nature, when there was so much genuine gladness that we had returned. Many of those who watched our ragged march had themselves experienced the same sort of hardships, and it was what we saw reflected in these men's eyes that really mattered.

My eyes travelled across the parade ground and over the roofs of the dockyard workshops towards the masts of the ships that lay alongside the wharves and basins of this great naval port. It was from here that seven months before — it seemed like seven years — that the proud new *Trinidad* had set out, resolved to get the Russian convoys through, whatever the cost might be. We had seen two outward convoys through, but at the cost of our cruiser and a saddening number of her ship's company.

We survivors who had now returned to our West Country Base, had gone through the horrible ordeal of naval warfare in the Arctic and all of us would be, more or less, marked by this for ever. The nerves of some were so shaken that they would not go to sea again, and others were so mutilated that they would not walk or see again. The boys had become men, while the men had quickly grown older. All of us, in the years to come, would be sure to go over in our minds, more than once, all the events which had interrupted our normally organised and often mundane lives.

One day this dreadful war would be over, and when it was, ships would be able to sail freely everywhere again. But by the time that the "Gateway to Hell" had been opened up, it would have cost the lives of 3,000 seamen of the Royal and Merchant Navies and 100 of their ships. Only the relentless Arctic hurricanes would continue to menace shipping. Leaving only the great white icebergs to sail in majesty over the silent unmarked graves of those who still remain there.

There would be moments, when the solitude of our thoughts would be disturbed by sounds and voices from the past. We would remember:-

The recurrent nerve jangling alarm bell, jerking us out of an exhausted sleep.

The urgent call over the speakers, "Action stations — Action".

The clanging steel as men raced up or down ladders to reach their posts.

Narrow gangways and spacious flats echoing to the sounds of cursing, running and half dressed men.

The nausea of sea-sickness, allied to weariness and numbing cold.

Enormous green seas, that scornfully tossed the great ship aside like a cork and then with giant hand smashed down upon it in brutish anger.

And far below, in lonely steel compartments, the eerie silence that followed the slamming of the great watertight doors, slotting into position, sealing water out, but sealing men in.

All these recollections of the grim days would be for ever carved upon the tablets of our memories.

But to most of us, the colouring of our memory would be overtoned with one colour — Grey; for we would remember grey ships, grey seas and grey skies but most of all — — Grey Men.

postscript

There were several matters which came to hand during my researches, that, though of a disjoined nature, are of sufficient interest and importance as to be worthy of a place in this book.

Several decorations were awarded for gallantry and devotion to duty as a result of these operations, including the D.S.O. to Captain Saunders, which award was intended to honour the whole ship's company. He also received a very kind letter from the Commander-in-Chief of the Home Fleet, Admiral Sir Jack Tovey, approving his conduct of the operations and commiserating with him on his cruel luck in the torpedoing of his ship.

One of the Polish passengers who survived the bombing on the return journey was a Mr. M. Kwapinski, on his way to take over the Polish Ministry of Industry and Commerce in London. He lost no time in telling the First Lord of the Admiralty and the Prime Minister of his admiration for the British Navy. His letter to Captain Saunders on his arrival in London ran as follows:-

"I am full of admiration for the splendid calm and extreme courage of all British sailors, even in moments of great distress."

Not all the fatalities of the Russian convoys were committed to the sea; a number were buried ashore at Murmansk in a cemetery on top of a small hill overlooking the port. The cemetery compound is surrounded by a low green wooden fence and by the gateway stands a memorial in Russian and English, reading:-

"This memorial was erected in memory of the warriors of the British Commonwealth of Nations and the United States of America, who brought help to the Soviet Union during the Patriotic War 1941–1945."

The graves with their granite headstones giving the names of the dead have been well cared for; and a small silver birch has been planted behind each of them.

Apart from this cemetery there is nothing in the city of

Murmansk to remind its people of the Allied wartime aid to Russia. The Museum, proudly shown off by guides, has an impressive section devoted to World War II. On one of the walls there are three pictures: of a lorry being loaded from a ship, of a tank coming to rest on a quay and an amphibious vehicle swinging from a crane in mid air. The lorry, the tank and the vehicle are all obviously American, to a Briton or an American. But the caption over the pictures read, "Even during the darkest days of the great Patriotic War, the heroic Soviet people continued to keep supplies flowing to the troops at the front". When someone pointed out that there was no mention of the Allied effort and help, the embarrassed guide replied, "Ah! but everyone knows that Britain and America helped us".

> *There is a comradeship of men, conceived in war,*
> *Which though impaired by time and space and age,*
> *Lives ever on.*
> *A bond, not made by ministers or kings,*
> *Nor penned by men of grand and high degree,*
> *To danger shared, a record writ in blood,*
> *Which only time and memory can dim.*

glossary

Barbette. Turret support.

Bosun's Yeoman. A rating assigned to the Bosun's stores.

Chief Buffer. Chief Bosun's mate, usually a Chief Petty Officer.

Closed up. At action stations.

Conned. Navigated.

Falls. The ropes on the davits where the ships boats are housed.

Flying Bridge. A long central elevated gangway from the bridge of a tanker over the decks.

Gash. Rubbish.

Gripes. Used to hold the ships boats in the davits.

Gunnery Rates. Gunnery ratings.

Jumping Wire. The stay wire which stretches fore and aft from the conning tower of a submarine.

Loading Numbers. Ratings who serve the guns.

Master at Arms. Senior rating, controlling lower deck organisation.

Pendant. Pennant, a tapering flag.

Ready Use Ammunition. Ammunition at hand ready for use.

Step the Mast. Rigging the mast.

Swifter. Rope.

Thompson Grab. An extension on the crane used for lifting the Walrus aircraft.

Weevils. Worms or grubs.